Restoring Antique Furniture
A Complete Guide

Richard A. Lyons

DOVER PUBLICATIONS, INC.
Mineola, New York

Bibliographical Note

This Dover edition, first published in 2000, is an unabridged, unaltered republication of *Complete Guide to Restoring Antique Furniture,* originally published in 1990 by Prentice-Hall, Inc., Englewood Cliffs, New Jersey.

Library of Congress Cataloging-in-Publication Data

Lyons, Richard A.
    Restoring antique furniture : a complete guide / Richard A. Lyons.
        p. cm.
    Reprint. Originally published: Englewood Cliffs, N.J. : Prentice Hall, c1990 under title: Complete guide to restoring antique furniture.
    ISBN 0-486-40954-6 (pbk.)
    1. Furniture—Repairing. 2. Furniture finishing. I. Lyons, Richard A. Complete guide to restoring antique furniture. II. Title.
TT199 .L89 2000
749'.1'0288—dc21
                                                            00-023154

Manufactured in the United States of America
Dover Publications, Inc., 31 East 2nd Street, Mineola, N.Y. 11501

Contents

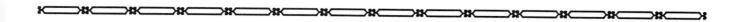

Introduction

Should the history of the human race be divided according to the achievements in the domestic arts, the period between 1600 and the mid-1800s would surely be the age of fine furniture. The quality of workmanship of that period has never been matched. With the arrival of the Industrial Revolution, which brought that era to a close, an entirely new approach to cabinetmaking developed. Every thing that demanded exactness and patience was eliminated, if possible. This "efficiency" led to a rapid decline in many of the crafts associated with fine furniture, such as the art of carving. From this an obsession grew to cut corners on workmanship and design. Windsor chair seats were made thinner, the mortise-and-tenon joint gave way to the inferior dowel joint, and wood of lower quality replaced the fine furniture woods.

Although the use of machines reduced the cost of furniture and made it widely available, the machine process has never matched the work of human hands. The fact is that machines do not allow us to be different. In handcrafted furniture, individuality can be seen even in work coming from the same hands. A variety of patterns said to be in the style of Chippendale are all different. Of all the ladder-back chairs I have seen, no set has been exactly the same as another set, and individual chairs within a set vary from each other. This "spirit" is absent from much of the furniture built after 1830.

It is difficult to pinpoint the exact time when we began to be satisfied with not having things of beauty around us. Perhaps it is the result of two terrible world wars in the first 50 years of this century. Perhaps it was the great depression between the two wars that dulled our appreciation for great homes and stunning furniture. In a conversation I had with a man who had been a clerk for an auctioneer during the Great Depression, he recalled times when an Ely Terry weight clock did not even get a bid, when tall four-poster beds were thrown on a scrap pile to go to ruin, and when the entire furnishings of a house were abandoned and left to the mercy of vandals. We do know that during the Great Depression, many householders could not afford to buy new furniture. This led the owners to paint or alter very fine pieces of early furniture. Finally, as drawers became so worn that they no longer functioned, joints became loose and weak, legs were broken, or tops became warped, a piece was discarded or relegated to the back porch.

By the end of World War II, many people had money for the first time in a number of years. As production returned to normal and the war effort came to a halt, consumer merchandise again became available. Probably to dismiss ourselves from the terrible past and move into a more promising future, everything old lost its appeal—"new" was the cry of the day. The general public seemed to have lost an appreciation for the beauty of home and furnishings so highly treasured by our forefathers. Nevertheless, there have always been those who saw the value of fine antique furniture, and much is owed to them for their efforts to preserve these treasures.

Despite the amount of furniture that was made in the seventeenth and eighteenth centuries, pieces from that period are difficult to find

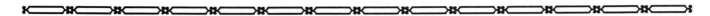

today. Occasionally, a fine example will surface, but it may not be in the best condition. I found an early Chippendale-style secretary being auctioned in a town in Indiana that was in such terrible condition that I barely recognized it for what it was. But I was able to rescue it and restore it. (Its restored condition is shown in Plate 6–2.) To find a fine example of early work and restore it to a new beginning is an experience that gives great satisfaction. From the classic styles, to the country style, to the primitive style, we have a tradition in furniture making of which we can all be proud.

It is the purpose of this book to encourage others to join in the quest. I believe that we owe it to our children and grandchildren to restore and preserve what remains of the fine furniture produced by our forefathers.

1

Rules and Tools for Restoration of Antique Furniture

Restoring, as the name implies, is the act of bringing something to its original condition. Restoring does not permit improving or changing, which means that the restorer must overcome the temptation to change the original, even if the change might add convenience. It would be unthinkable, for example, to replace a worn turnbuckle with a magnetic latch, or to replace a warped or cracked board at the back of a cupboard with a piece of plywood. Such changes would greatly reduce the value of the piece.

If learning what restoring means is the first step in working with antique furniture, the second is surely learning when a piece of furniture is worth restoring. That decision depends on the purpose in saving the piece. If a person is restoring a piece of furniture because it is solid wood and can be used, then almost any solid wood piece is worth the effort. In most cases, it will be less expensive to restore an old piece than to buy a new one, and the old one will be of better quality. For the most part, the furniture produced in this country today is made of poorer woods than in earlier times, and it is stapled together, its drawers are assembled with butt joints and super-glue, and little craftsmanship goes into the design.

If an item is to be restored because it is an heirloom, nothing else about the piece has any bearing on the decision. Whether or not the piece has antique value does not matter because the prime purpose is to preserve a part of a family's history so that it can be enjoyed by future generations. Of all the reasons for restoring, this is probably the most noble—but here we may find

our greatest challenges because some of these pieces may be in such poor condition that the owner is about to abandon them. The Shaker table shown in Plate 6–9, for example, was on a trash truck headed for a landfill when it was rescued.

If a piece is being considered for restoration because of its possible antique value, the decision becomes more complicated. One important factor here is its overall condition. That is, if as much as one-fourth of the principal parts are missing, the true value is lost. If a single major part (say, a carved skirt on a Queen Anne highboy) is missing, the antique value will be reduced considerably. However, if excellent craftsmanship can be employed and the part replaced with old wood, then the piece should be restored. Obviously, this course of action will enable future generations to enjoy the piece, and if the work is done well enough, *it may not even be detectable* by the inexperienced eye.

Rules of Restoration

Once the decision has been made to restore a piece, the next step is to go over the basic procedure, keeping in mind the following rules:

1. Repairs should be made from wood of the same age and type.
2. As little of the original stock should be removed as possible.

3

3. Any natural breaks in the design should be utilized as a starting point for a repair.

4. Damaged areas on a veneered surface should be repaired with irregularly shaped patches.

5. If the design of a piece depends on the feet for proper proportion and the feet are badly worn or missing, it is best to undertake major repair and restore it to the correct proportions.

6. No part should be discarded until the restoration is complete, as it may hold a clue to the original structure.

7. When a piece is found that has parts missing, the immediate surroundings should be searched before the piece is taken home. Otherwise, the part may be sold to someone else in another lot of merchandise.

Tools to Use in the Restoration Process

Occasionally, I obtain a very fine piece of furniture that provides such a unique challenge that I do the restoration using only the tools that were available at the time the piece was constructed. But for the most part I use modern tools in my restoration efforts. I feel comfortable

with this because I am sure that the old masters would have used the table saw, band saw, surfacer, and other tools had they been available. If modern tools are used in restoration, care should be taken to remove any modern tool marks from the work. If I use a modern surfacer I never reduce the stock down to the finished thickness, but instead finish the task with a 14-inch smoothing plane (see Plate 1–1). If a rabbet joint is needed, I will cut it to near size on the table saw, and then use a rabbet plane to complete the work. By virtue of the unique structure of the rabbet plane, it can serve many purposes. The blade of the rabbet plane extends the full width of the bed of the plane. This allows the craftsperson to work in close corners. The rabbet plane is also shown in Plate 1–1. To smooth out rough end-grain surfaces, I use a low-angle block plane. The one shown in Plate 1–1 has a blade that is set at about 22 degrees. This low angle allows the blade to encounter the wood at such a low angle that it shaves the wood fibers. This reduces the chance of splintering any edge grain and provides a surface that can be sanded smooth rather easily. All the tools shown in Plate 1–1 were obtained at auction. I bought these at a time when the old wooden planes were the only tools commanding high prices. Consequently, I was able to obtain all the tools shown at a very modest price. The fourth tool from the left in Plate 1–1 is a spoke shave. It is actually a wheelwright's tool, but it serves wonderfully well as

PLATE 1–1

From left to right, 14 inch smoothing plane, rabbet plane, block plane, spoke shave, reeding tool.

PLATE 1–2

Example of early molding planes.

a cabinetmaker's tool. It can be used to smooth concave curves and plane out other odd contoured edges. The tool on the far right in Plate 1–1 is a beading tool. This is a rather rare tool. It has four small blades that are half-round concave in shape. Some of the blades have four such shapes, while others have two or even just one such concave shape. This tool allows me to reproduce the edge beading and fluting so common on early furniture. It is one of my most prized tools. I am sure that there must be many beading tools in existence, but this is the only one I have ever seen available for sale. Its rarity was recognized by several persons at the auction where I obtained it, and I had to pay a rather handsome price to become its owner.

Plate 1–2 shows four wooden molding planes. Although I have many such planes, these four seem to be the ones that always end up on the workbench when I am in the process of duplicating a molding. A very fine craftsman, William Edward Arnold of Louisville, Kentucky, presented this complete set of planes to me many years ago. Mr. Arnold was a person very much concerned with keeping the art of furniture making alive.

Plate 1–3 illustrates the type of wood chisel that I use. The ones shown are called socket chisels because of the way the handles are affixed to the chisel. You can see that they are not a matched set. These chisels were bought one at a time at auctions whenever the opportunity pre-

sented itself. With these chisels and a wooden mallet, many things can be done. I use the smaller chisels to dig out mortises for mortise-and-tenon joints, while the wider chisels are used to cut mortises to set hinges or trim out stock. I prefer the long chisel, as it gives better leverage.

Some simple rules to follow when using wood chisels are:

1. Always keep the chisels sharp.
2. Always secure all stock with a clamp when using a chisel.
3. Always keep both hands behind the cutting end of the tool.

PLATE 1–3

Group of wood chisels.

PLATE 1–4
MEASURING TOOLS

From left to right, sliding T bevel, 6 inch square, marking guage, 24 inch bench rule.

Plate 1–4 illustrates some measuring devices that are necessary for any cabinetmaker. The sliding T-bevel makes it possible to transfer angles. The 6-inch square is one of the first tools that I bought when I started building my tool chest, and is excellent for small work. I use a large framing square for larger work. The marking gauge is indispensible for laying out for hinge placement and mortise-and-tenon joints. The 24-inch bench rule serves well for furniture work.

These are my most used tools. They are like old friends. No matter what I am working on, by the end of the day the tools I have discussed always seem to end up on the workbench.

My power tools include a lathe, a band saw, a joiner, a table saw, a scroll saw, a radial arm saw, and a surfacer. I use these tools extensively. However, as mentioned earlier, I make sure that all modern tool marks are removed from all surfaces when the piece of furniture is being completely restored. This includes surfaces that are hidden. I hasten to say that I do not remove modern tool marks with the intent to deceive. I remove all modern tool marks to return the work to its original condition. In fact, I sign all my restoration efforts. I believe that in time my signed restored work will have more value than trying to deceive someone in the present.

Caring for Tools

I have found it is best to have power saw blades, joiner knives, and planer knives sharpened by professionals. These persons have the equipment to provide uniform edges for the knives, and the correct set and pitch for the saw blades. But I prefer to sharpen hand tools myself. It would be a real problem always to be taking the hand-plane blades and chisels elsewhere for sharpening, due to the turnaround time and cost. With a little practice most people can master the art of sharpening hand tools.

The craftsperson will need a grinding wheel, a good oilstone, and a square. The grinding wheel may be either fast wheel or slow turning. A fast wheel (about 3600 rpm) works well, but you must be careful not to hold a tool to the wheel too long. This can get the tool edge hot and cause it to lose its temper. If this happens, the tool will not be able to hold a cutting edge. There is a slow-speed grinder on the market that has one wheel for grinding and a second wheel for honing. If a craftsperson has some concern about using a fast wheel, he or she should investigate the purchase of the slower wheel.

A cutting edge needs grinding only if it shows nicks or is not square. If an edge seems smooth, and you are not certain if honing is needed, there is a simple solution: Hold the cutting edge to the light. If you can see a shiny beaded edge, the blade is dull. If this is the case, honing the cutting edge on an oilstone will return a good sharp edge.

The tool rest on the grinding wheel is set to give a grind angle of 20 to 30 degrees. I prefer an angle close to 20 degrees.

Sharpening the Blade of a Hand Plane

A note on terminology seems in order here. The part of the plane that does the cutting is called the plane iron or plane blade. The part that is secured to the plane iron by a large-headed screw is called the plane iron cap. The cap helps to stiffen the blade or iron, and also bends the wood shavings up so they will clear the plane.

Step 1. Remove the blade from the plane iron cap by loosening the screw that holds the two pieces together. Turn the two pieces 90 degrees to one another. Slide the plane iron cap down the slot in the blade and let the large screwhead come through the large hole at the end of the slot (see Plates 1–5 and 1–6).

Step 2. Check the cutting edge of the blade to determine if it is square, as shown in Plate 1–7.

PLATE 1–5

Loosening the plane iron-cap screw.

PLATE 1–6

Separating the plane iron cap from the plane blade.

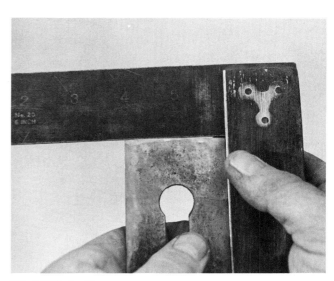

PLATE 1–7

Checking the plane blade for square.

Note: If the reader has never sharpened a plane blade before, it might be wise to secure an old blade and do a little practicing.

In the following discussion, it can be seen that the wheel guard has been removed in order to obtain a better view. The operator should always keep the wheel guard in its proper position, and wear eye protection.

Step 3. Turn the grinding wheel on and with the plane blade held firmly on the tool rest, start grinding with one side of the blade positioned about center of the wheel.

Step 4. Holding the pressure constant on the wheel, move the blade across the wheel until the complete cutting edge has been ground. The progression of cut is shown in Plates 1–8 to 1–10, moving from left to right.

Step 5. Check the ground edge with a square and see if all the nicks have been removed. If not, make another pass. Do this until the cutting edge is free of nicks and is square.

PLATE 1–8
Starting the first pass.

PLATE 1–9
Half way across the face of the wheel.

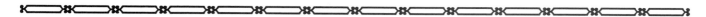

PLATE 1–10

Completion of the pass.

Step 6. After the cutting edge has been properly ground, it must be honed on the oilstone.

Honing a Cutting Edge on an Oilstone

Step 1. Place a small quantity of mineral oil on the flat stone.

Step 2. Place the blade at a very low angle to the surface with the beveled side down.

Step 3. Raise the blade slowly until the mineral oil is pushed out from under the beveled portion of the blade. This will indicate that you have the blade at the proper angle on the oilstone. This is shown in Plate 1–11a.

Step 4. Holding the blade at that angle, move it over the surface of the stone in a figure-eight motion. This motion will cause the oilstone to wear evenly.

Step 5. Turn the blade over and place it flat against the oilstone (Plate 1–11b). Move it backward and forward to remove any metal residue that might be on the edge. It may be necessary to repeat steps 4 and 5 several times to remove this metal residue, commonly called a "wire edge." If you have been successful in

PLATE 1–11a

Positioning the beveled edge on the oilstone.

PLATE 1–11b

Removing the metal residue from the iron.

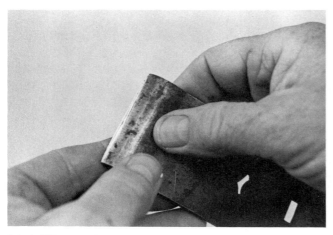

PLATE 1–12

Positioning the plane iron with the plane iron cap.

your attempt to sharpen the blade, it should slice through a sheet of suspended paper.

Step 6. Reassemble the plane blade with the plane iron by holding the two pieces at a 90-degree angle and place the large screwhead in the hole at the end of the slot.

Step 7. Slide the plane iron up far enough in the slot so that it will not hit the cutting edge when it is rotated around to align with the plane blade.

Step 8. Position the plane blade so that the cutting edge protrudes past the end of the cap iron about the thickness of a dime (see Plate 1–12).

Step 9. Tighten the cap-iron screw securely and place the blade assembly back into the plane frame.

Sharpening a Wood Chisel

The wood chisel can be sharpened in exactly the same manner that the plane blade is sharpened. For heavy work, I prefer to set the bevel on the cutting edge at about 30 degrees. When I am doing very light shaving or carving, I prefer the bevel to be about 20 degrees. How you sharpen your chisel will depend on your own preference.

Maintaining Other Tools

Since I have my table saw blades, joiner knives, and planer knives sharpened commercially, the only other maintenance that I am concerned with is directed toward keeping tools clean and handles tight, and, of course, general maintenance.

Finishing

Earliest examples of furniture indicate that some type of finish was used, with decoration being the primary purpose. As the use of furniture developed, the need for protection became apparent. Beeswax, paint, and oil were probably the earliest forms of finish. Paint was a popular form of finish in that it was relatively low in cost, and in the case of the early colonials, it provided some color in their otherwise rather drab surroundings. Honey was a common staple, and with honey came beeswax. It was noted that bees sealed their hives by laying down a coat of wax. From this came the idea of rubbing furniture with beeswax to provide protection. The kitchen worktable in William Shakespeare's home is an excellent example of the kind of finish that can be obtained by applying beeswax. An early method was to rub the wood with cork saturated in wax—a method that required many hours of hard work. Later, beeswax dissolved in turpentine applied with a cloth proved easier and equally effective. In the eighteenth century, shellac became a common finishing product. When shellac is used it should be brushed on in very thin layers, with 48 hours of drying time between each layer. The work must be hand rubbed between layers. Oil provides an excellent protection if a slight darkening of the surface is not objectionable. Oil penetrates deep into wood and is rather easily repaired when the finish is damaged. It can be applied with a cloth, and a clean environment is not essential. When oil is used, two or three days may pass between applying coats. As a tabletop shows wear or dryness, oil may be applied again. This can go on for

years. By doing this a wonderful deep finish will build on the wood. Varnish has been used in France for many years but was not used extensively in the United States until about 1900. Varnish is applied with a brush, and due to the rather long drying time, the environment must be very clean.

Preparing for Finishing

In restoring old surfaces, care should be used in coloring any material that is to be used to fill in imperfections. Sawdust from the same wood mixed with glue makes a good filler material. The use of putty should be avoided. If a large imperfection exists, fit a plug from the same type of wood in the damaged area. Do not sand old surfaces. You will take away from the value of the work.

If the old finish must be removed, use a paint or varnish remover. These products will not damage the patina. Those of us who have used commercial paint and varnish remover know that the dissolved finish forms a rather repulsive paste. To remove this dissolved finish from the wood requires many rags or a coarse steel wool. I have found that by applying generous portions of remover, the paste becomes rather liquid. If the person doing the refinishing will then cover the surface with sawdust from the table saw, and rub briskly with rags or a soft bristle brush, most of the old finish will be absorbed into the sawdust. The sawdust can then be discarded. The secret to this technique is to apply enough remover to make the dissolved finish somewhat liquid. This drastically reduces the need for rags and steel wool. If the finish being removed is shellac, after removal, the surface should be cleaned with No. 000 steel wool saturated with denatured alcohol. This will remove all film from the surface without harming the wood. If the finish being removed is varnish, go over the surface with No. 000 steel wool saturated in mineral spirits. Carving, turns, and other irregular surfaces should be cleaned with great gentleness. A discarded toothbrush serves the purpose admirably.

I hesitate even to mention the next item

and strongly recommend against its use. Nevertheless, a quick, cheap way to strip a surface is by dipping the work in lye water. This method will damage the surface of the wood by raising the grain and will darken the surface of woods such as cherry, walnut, and mahogany.

Refurbishing Old Finishes

Shellac. Since shellac will dissolve in denatured alcohol, it is easy to restore a worn shellac finish. Working in an area that is not seen, apply alcohol to the surface with a clean brush. Work the surface until the shellac has returned to liquid. Once you have experimented with this process and feel that you understand what is happening, work over the entire piece. Work with the surfaces horizontal, if possible. After the entire surface has been reworked, allow the shellac to dry. Using No. 000 steel wool, rub the surface down. You may wish to add one coat of new shellac. Do all of this in a dry environment. Alcohol will absorb water. If the environment is humid, the finish will haze.

Varnish. Varnish will not redissolve into liquid form. Therefore, it is difficult to restore a dark, cracked varnish finish. You can remove all wax with mineral spirits, and then rub the surface with No. 000 steel wool. Follow this with two or three applications of linseed oil. I prefer to heat the oil to a temperature that can be tolerated with the bare hand.

As you refinish, do not over restore or prepare the surface. Leave as many legitimate wear features as possible, repairing only what is necessary for the piece of furniture to be functional. Remember that this is an antique. It is old, and should look old. People who have the urge to bring an old piece to a like-new condition would be better off having someone build a reproduction of the work.

Finishing Environment

If refinishing involves shellac or varnish, the environment must be clean and dust free. Ideally, the air should be rather dry and warm (60 percent or lower humidity and 70°F or higher tempera-

ture). The work should be done in natural light, if possible. If artificial light is used, there should be a great deal of it. Although I do not feel that spray finishes have a place in restoration, they must be considered. If the finish is applied with a spray gun, caution must be taken to avoid open flame. There must be excellent ventilation, and the craftsperson must wear an approved respirator.

Finishing Tips

Avoid a high-gloss finish. Early furniture simply did not carry such a finish, and to apply a glossy finish will only reduce the value of the piece. Unseen surfaces of a piece of furniture need to be sealed with shellac or varnish. This is particularly true for tabletops and leaves. I own a hammer dulcimer in which the lid is a single walnut board, with the underside veneered to provide a beautiful panel when the instrument is open. The top surface of the lid is not veneered, and consequently, gains and loses moisture rather easily. Due to the unequal breathing capability of the two surfaces, the top is badly dished. All efforts to flatten the top and seal the outer surface to equalize the moisture movement have failed. By the same token, if a deep finish is placed on the upper surface of a tabletop while leaving the undersurface bare, the top will probably warp.

Finishes should be applied with all brass removed. Stains should be used only when trying to blend a repair into the surrounding surface. The natural color of wood varies. The same tree may incorporate several different colors of wood, depending on whether a particular board came from near the center of the tree or near the outside surface. There were enough fine-quality trees for our forefathers to select not only which tree to use but which part of the tree. It is difficult for those of us living today to imagine the abundance of trees in the United States as late as 1880. My grandfather told me that when the leaves of the wild cherry tree fell after the first killing frost of the fall, they were poisonous to cows. Therefore, it was a common practice to cut all the cherry trees on their dairy farm and burn them. He recalled cherry trees laying on the ground whose diameters were so great that as a young boy he could not see over the trunks. It is easy to see that with such an availability of trees, early furniture was made from stock well matched in color.

As the supply of such fine trees diminished, the cabinetmaker became less particular as to the choice of stock. Therefore, expect to find some country furniture where sapwoods do show. Nevertheless, I would not recommend staining. Let the natural beauty of the wood remain evident.

2

Keys to the Treasures

Although some of the characteristics described in this chapter apply to any antique piece, the primary interest here is antique American furniture and its distinctive features. To begin with, most American-made furniture can be classified into three groups: classical, country, and primitive. Classical furniture—which includes Sheraton, Hepplewhite, Queen Anne, Chippendale, and Adams Brothers—was usually made in small well-equipped shops under the direct supervision of a master craftsman. Extreme care was given to the selection of materials and techniques of construction. Furniture of this type will have turns, carvings, and curves.

Country furniture has straighter lines and simpler designs and is more functional than classical furniture. It, too, is superbly constructed. In this case, however, it is usually the work of one outstanding craftsman who had relatively few tools and materials. Many of these persons were journeymen who had completed their apprenticeship and had set out on their own. To avoid competing with established tradesmen, they often went into the frontier villages and towns and there built furniture as the need arose. If the towns were large enough to support the trade, a journeyman would settle, build a shop, and construct a lathe. Thus early country furniture may have turned legs, posts, and drawer pulls.

Primitive furniture, meanwhile, can be described as the product of a need. It was constructed with little skill and meager tools, usually nothing more than a saw, hammer, and a few nails. Primitive work is often out of square and ill-conceived, but it manages to be functional.

Although in some respects primitive furniture cannot compare with good country furniture and certainly not with finely constructed classical pieces, it has a certain charm that makes it just as collectible as other types.

Evaluating a piece of furniture for its antique value requires close attention to certain details: the construction technique, the materials used, the tool signature, and the hardware. Antique American furniture will be made of cherry, walnut, maple, poplar, pine, oak, and mahogany. Good early mahogany is dark reddish brown, dense, and heavy, and it has a straight grain with narrow sapwood. The source for this fine wood was Santo Domingo (now the Dominican Republic), but the supply was exhausted by 1820. Mahogany from other sources—principally Honduras, Mexico, Africa, and India—then came into use, but it was inferior in color and texture. Basically, the quality of the mahogany can be judged by its weight; if it is heavy, it is good. Because Santo Domingan mahogany is such a rare wood, pieces made from it should be cherished.

Construction Joints

In examining a piece of furniture to determine its age, the best place to start is a drawer, if drawers are available. The oldest pieces with dovetail construction will have a double-pin dovetail to secure the sides to the front (Figure 2–1a). This type of construction has the undesirable trait of allowing the front of the drawer to

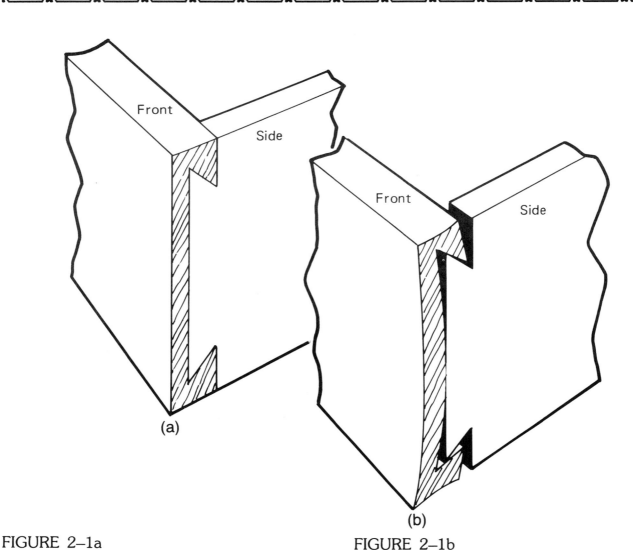

FIGURE 2–1a

Early dovetail drawer construction consisting of a double-pin dovetail.

FIGURE 2–1b

The double-pin dovetail allows the drawer front to warp.

warp (Figure 2–1b). Because of this problem, drawers were soon made with three or more pin dovetails. If the dovetails and pins are equal in width and are uniformly spaced, however, the joints are probably machine made, and should be considered modern (Figure 2–2). Handmade dovetail joints will be unequal in size and shape, and will often show scribe lines where they were laid out individually (Figure 2–3).

A fine classical piece will have dovetail con-struction in all its drawers. Although dovetail construction is common in country furniture, the dado joint held with square nails is also common and an acceptable feature. Dovetail construction is seldom found in primitive work.

The drawers on old furniture will have a bottom consisting of a single board, or two boards joined by an unglued tongue and groove. Except in primitive work, the drawer bottom will be beveled at the edges and fitted in a groove

in the sides and front of the drawer (Figure 2–4a). In primitive work the bottom of the drawer may be nailed or pegged to the bottom edge of the drawer sides and back (Figure 2–4b).

Framing joints can tell a great deal about the skill of a craftsperson. Never expect to see nails as a major fastener in examples of classical furniture. Country and primitive pieces are the only types in which nails can be justified as the major means of holding the piece together. All good classical furniture and much country furniture will feature a liberal use of dovetails, mortise-and-tenon joints, dado joints, and variations of these joints. The dovetail joint is used in framing because of its great strength—any attempt to pull it apart will merely tighten the wedge. The open dovetail, the half dovetail, and the open dovetail lap joint are commonly found in old furniture and serve as good indicators of its age and the quality of construction. (Figure 2–5 illustrates the use of the dovetail in framing.)

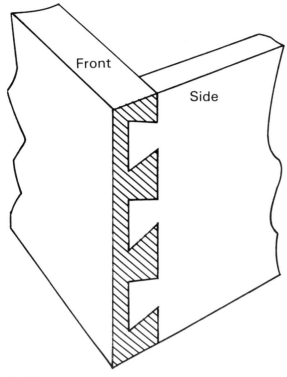

FIGURE 2–2

Dovetail construction showing pins and dovetails of equal size can be considered machine made and therefore modern.

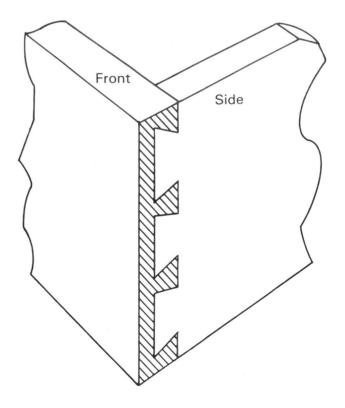

FIGURE 2–3

Dovetail construction with wide dovetails and narrow pins unequal in size and shape and with evidence of scribe lines are handmade; if other features suggesting age are present, the piece can be considered old.

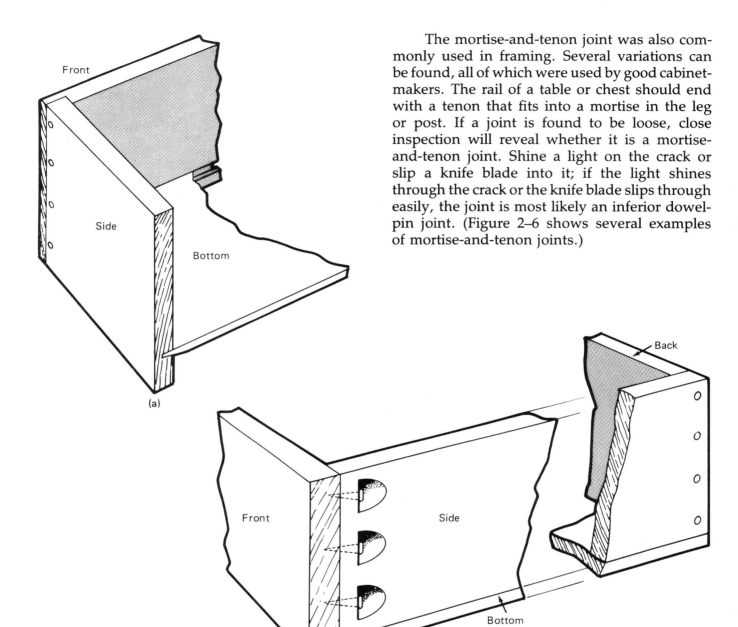

The mortise-and-tenon joint was also commonly used in framing. Several variations can be found, all of which were used by good cabinetmakers. The rail of a table or chest should end with a tenon that fits into a mortise in the leg or post. If a joint is found to be loose, close inspection will reveal whether it is a mortise-and-tenon joint. Shine a light on the crack or slip a knife blade into it; if the light shines through the crack or the knife blade slips through easily, the joint is most likely an inferior dowel-pin joint. (Figure 2–6 shows several examples of mortise-and-tenon joints.)

FIGURE 2–4a

The dado joint with square nails is an accepted construction feature in some country furniture and in all primitive work. Notice that the bottom of the drawer fits in a groove around the sides and front; this is a common feature in classical and country furniture.

FIGURE 2–4b

The drawer construction using the butt joint and recessed nails is very old and primitive. Notice that the bottom is secured to the bottom edge of the sides and back; this is an accepted feature. The author has seen only one example of this type of drawer construction that was unquestionably old. It is very rare.

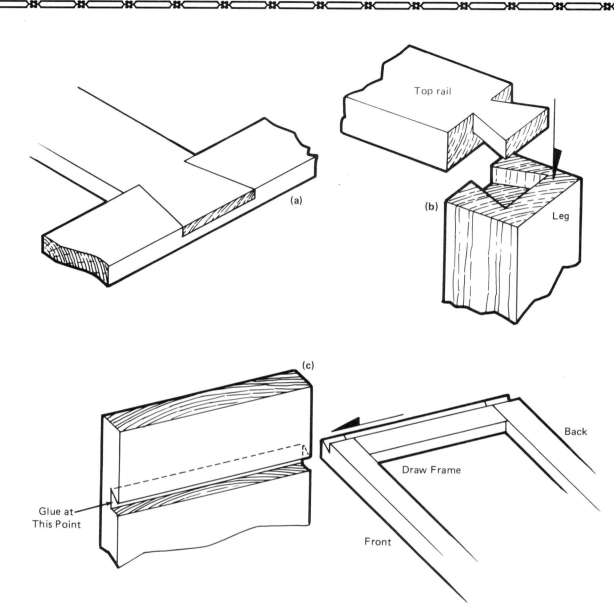

(a)

(b) Top rail Leg

(c)

Glue at This Point

Back

Draw Frame

Front

FIGURE 2–5a
DOVETAIL LAP JOINT

The dovetail lap joint was used extensively in securing members of a frame construction.

FIGURE 2–5b
OPEN DOVETAIL LAP JOINT

An excellent way to secure the top drawer frame to the leg of a step table.

FIGURE 2–5c
HALF DOVETAIL JOINT

Used by good cabinetmakers, and a highly desirable construction feature. The frame was glued to the end piece at the front or exposed edge to maintain alignment and then left unglued along the length, but had a tight fit. As the solidboard end expands and contracts, the frame will slide in the groove. If the frame was glued to the end board along the entire length of the joint, the expansion and contraction of the end would cause it to split.

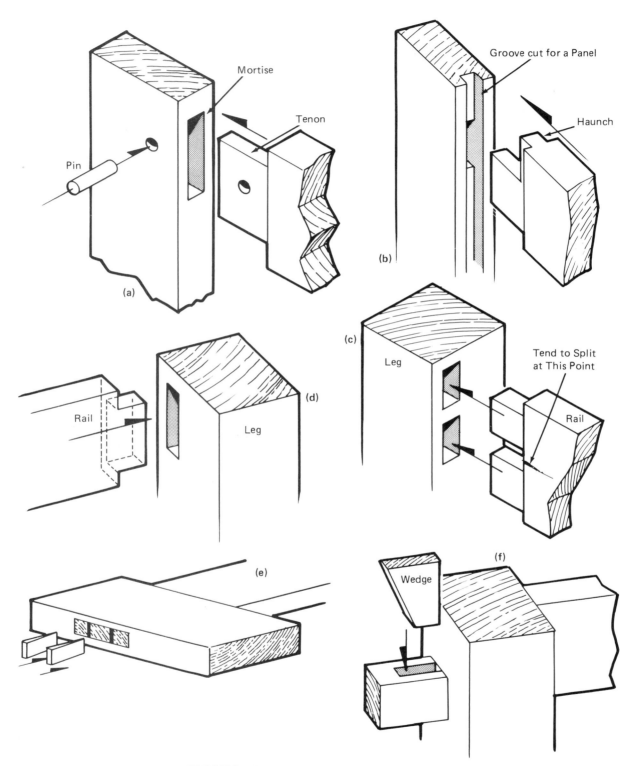

FIGURE 2–6
TYPES OF MORTISE TENON JOINTS

FIGURE 2–6a
BLIND MORTISE AND TENON WITH PIN

A very strong joint, and time consuming to make by hand.

FIGURE–2–6b
HAUNCHED MORTISE AND TENON JOINT

Used on paneled doors. The haunch fills the groove cut for the panel, which was allowed to run the full length of the rail.

FIGURE 2–6c
DOUBLE MORTISE AND TENON

The double mortise and tenon may be pinned or haunched. This is a very strong joint and is difficult to cut. The major disadvantage is that the rail will split between the two tenons if it is very wide because when the rail expands and contracts the tenons will not be able to move.

FIGURE 2–6d
BAREFACED MORTISE AND TENON

When the rails and legs of a piece are made flush, very little wood is left between the mortise and the face of the leg if a regular tenon is used. To strengthen the joint, the tenon is made on the inside face of the rail.

FIGURE 2–6e
WEDGED MORTISE AND TENON

A through mortise and tenon can be given added strength by cutting slits in the tenon before it is assembled, and by driving wedges into the slits afterward.

FIGURE 2–6f
KEYED MORTISE AND TENON

This provides a very strong and tight joint, yet it is easy to dissemble. Used on large tables that were only needed for special occasions and could be disassembled and stored when not in use.

If a piece of furniture is constructed with pinned mortise-and-tenon joints, a clue to its age will be found in these joints. If the pin is protruding from the face of the stock in which it is driven, the piece is in all likelihood relatively old. Such a protrusion develops when the pin is driven across the grain and through the years the stock has shrunk whereas the length of the pin has remained unchanged (see Plate 2–1).

In the dowel joint, two or more pins extending from the end of a rail fit into holes bored in the legs or post of a piece of furniture (Figure 2–7). This joint is inferior to the mortise-and-tenon joint in both strength and holding capabilities. Since it was an easy way to avoid cutting the more expensive mortise-and-tenon joint, the

PLATE 2–1
PINNED MORTISE AND TENON

The protrusion of the pins from the surface of the leg of this panel-and-post blanket chest is extreme. The blanket chest was found in a barn and was being used for a feed storage box. It is made of cherry, and the surface is nearly black with age.

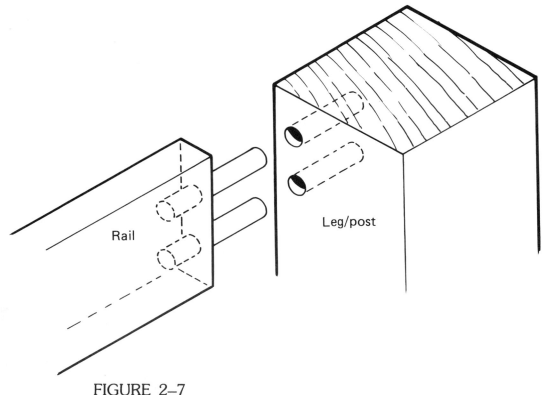

FIGURE 2–7
TWO-PIN DOWEL JOINT

An inferior technique for securing rails to legs. A weak attempt at replacing the mortise-and-tenon joint.

dowel joint quickly became popular and by the early twentieth century was in wide use. First used in cheap furniture, it soon found its way into supposedly good expensive furniture. Whatever the case, it is a fairly reliable indicator of the age of a piece.

Turns

Columns, spindles, and other types of turns have been favorite forms of decoration for centuries. The lathe, which is the oldest type of woodworking machine, made it possible to bring beauty and style to the simplest piece of furniture through the use of well-turned forms (Figure 2–8a). Of course, the key phrase here is well turned, since a poorly turned spindle can destroy the beauty of a good piece.

Initially, turns were made by holding the tool in the hand. The design was limited only by the skill of the turner. Early turners worked with crude measuring devices and depended primarily on the eye to determine when the work was properly shaped. Therefore, it is not uncommon to find that the legs of an early table are not identical. Furthermore, good hand-turned work can be expected to show considerable differences between the smallest diameter and the largest diameter within a design. The technique of undercutting was used to form the concave surface of the design (Figure 2–8b).

Because turning by hand is time consuming and expensive, a technique called *machine turning*

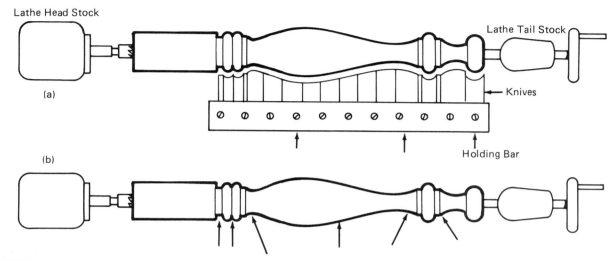

FIGURE 2–8a
MACHINE TURNING

The tool holder grips seventeen separate knives in a holding bar. Only in-and-out movement can take place at 90 degrees to the axis of the work.

FIGURE 2–8b
HAND TURNING

Hand turning allows the cutting tool to approach the stock from many angles, and thus gives the craftsman greater freedom in forming the contour of the work.

was developed. Machine turning replaces the person as the toolholder with a clamping device that can hold several cutting tools that have been ground to form the desired pattern. The toolholder is capable of moving toward and away from the stock to be turned at a 90-degree angle only, and cut the full length of the pattern in one motion. This technique of cutting the entire stock at one time placed considerable strain on the wood and thus made it impractical to cut very small diameters, since the stock could break. As a result, the free-flowing designs so characteristic of hand work had to be avoided. In addition, since the angle of cutting was fixed, undercutting could not be used, much to the detriment of the overall design. Remember, machine-turned pieces have the following characteristics:

1. There are no signs of undercutting.
2. Free-flowing designs that emphasize the contrast between larger and smaller diameters are absent.
3. All turnings within a set are identical in size and shape.

Look at Figure 2–8, which illustrates the difference between hand turning and machine turning. Now turn to Plate 2–2, which shows four table legs, and let us see what we can determine about their construction. The set from which the leg on the far left was taken had legs identical in size and shape. This fact plus the absence of undercutting strongly suggests that this leg was machine turned.

The second and third legs from the left were probably hand turned; the large section—a simple round piece in one case and a square in the other—was an early style used to reduce the turning time for the legs. Note, too, that the overall design of the second leg from the left is rather poor. The third leg from the left does show good movement in the turn, what little there is left of it. The leg on the right is from a very old piece. Notice the drastic difference in the diameters here. Also notice that the undercutting is deep and well done. The legs in the set from which this one came were all slightly different in size.

PLATE 2–2
EXAMPLE OF TURNS

The poorest example is the leg on the extreme left; the better turn is on the extreme right.

Carvings

In early pieces the carving was reserved for the master craftsman, never the apprentice. The work of such persons is characterized by its deep undercutting, which contrasts sharply with the raised edges. Close examination will also reveal slight differences in seemingly identical carvings. Like turning, hand carving gave way to machines and was on its way out by 1830. By 1910, the press technique was in wide use, as can be seen from the large number of press-back chairs that have come down from that period. Press carving, a term that is really a misnomer, is easily recognized by the shallowness of the pattern and the broken fiber wherever the press crushed the wood.

Materials

Another important point to note about the construction of early pieces is the wood used. Colonial America had an abundance of huge trees that provided wood well suited to furniture. The wide boards produced by these trees made it unnecessary to edge-glue two or more narrow boards together to obtain desired width. If a craftsman of the eighteenth century needed a 23-inch tabletop, it would be a matter of selecting a tree large enough to produce such boards. In contrast, the craftsman of today would have to glue two or three boards edge to edge to obtain the desired width. Thus it can be seen how the presence of very wide boards in furniture help determine the construction date.

Those large trees have been gone for many years; thus, when a piece of furniture is found to be constructed of boards of this size, every effort should be made to preserve it. A prime example is a six-board blanket chest. The chest derives its name from the fact that a single board forms the top, front, both ends, and the bottom. The chest is normally constructed with dovetail joints at the corners, and not a single edge-to-edge glue joint is used in the entire piece.

Once trees of this size disappeared, edge gluing became necessary to obtain desired widths. Because different techniques have evolved here as well, the way that boards are glued together will provide further clues to the date of the work. The early glue joints were simple butt joints; early in the twentieth century the tongue-and-groove joint was widely used; and around 1950 the rule joint was introduced

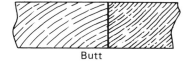 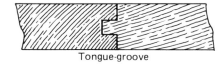 

| Butt | Tongue-groove | Rule Joint |

FIGURE 2–9

GLUE JOINTS

The butt joint on the left is the oldest and simplest method of gluing boards edge to edge. The tongue-and-groove joint (center) appeared next in furniture making, and the rule joint is the most modern.

(Figure 2–9). Even though both the tongue-and-groove joint and the rule joint are superior to the butt joint, they should never be used when restoring a very old piece of furniture.

Stretchers and Rails

Stretchers and rails used on tables and chests in the seventeenth century were made flush with the surface of the legs or post. This technique required extra attention to fitting and finishing, but was common practice by the craftsman of that time. By 1840 it became common to set the rails in slightly from the outside surface of the legs and post. This was yet another shortcut introduced in furniture making to save time since it meant that an exact fit did not have to be made. You should certainly be aware of this detail, but do not discount the value of a piece of furniture carrying an offset rail. Just be more appreciative of the pieces that have flush rails. (Both types of construction are shown in Figure 2–10.)

The rod stretchers on chairs hold further clues to the age of a chair. The stretcher on older chairs will usually have a knob cut on the ends, whereas the stretcher on more modern chairs will have a smooth end (Figure 2–11). The stock for the stretchers on old chairs was well seasoned, but that for the legs was not completely seasoned. The chair would be assembled without

FIGURE 2–10a

FLUSH CONSTRUCTION

Flush construction requires a barefaced mortise-and-tenon joint. This type of work takes great skill and care.

FIGURE 2–10b

OFFSET CONSTRUCTION

The offset allowed for the use of a regular mortise-and-tenon joint, and provided some margin of error.

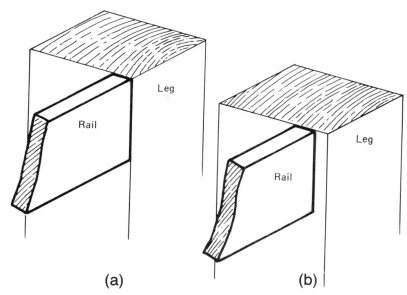

(a)   (b)

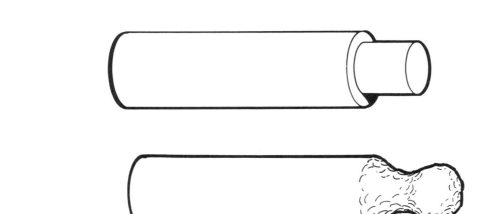

FIGURE 2–11
CHAIR STRETCHERS

The stretcher illustrated on the top is a typical modern stretcher. The knob on the stretcher shown on the bottom indicates a much earlier work. These knobs were often formed by whittleing with a knife.

glue, and allowed to set until the stock of the unseasoned leg dried. As it dried, it would shrink and close in around the knob on the end of the stretcher, thereby making an extremely tight joint. This construction technique often puzzles people who are trying to rework an old chair today. The chair will be loose at every joint and look as though it is ready to fall apart, yet it will be very difficult to actually disassemble.

Tool Marks

Hand tools, the lathe included, are known to have existed as far back as early Egyptian times, but manpower remained the only means of operating woodworking tools until the nineteenth century. As late as 1790 there were only two ways to reduce a log to flat boards. It was either sawed with a pit saw or rived.

A board was rived by means of a dull tool called a froe, which was forced into the end of the log. Being very dull, the tool would cause the wood to split along the natural path of the grain rather than across the grain fibers. Depending on the desired thickness, the froe was moved over and once again driven into the end of the log. If the grain was true, a board would be produced. Most of the seats of early Windsor chairs were made from riving stock and carry the signature of the riving process on the under-

side (see Plate 2–3). (The riving process is illustrated in Figure 2–12.)

The pit saw, as the name implies, was operated from a pit dug into the earth. A wood frame was constructed across the pit and a log placed on the frame and secured from rolling. One person (the tiller) stood on top of the log and one person stood under the log. Using an up-and-down motion to operate a large saw similar to a cross-cut saw, they sawed logs into boards (Figure 2–13). The signature of the pit saw consists of kerf marks that vary in width and in the angle at which they cross the grain (see

PLATE 2–3

SIGNATURE OF THE RIVEN PROCESS

The bottom of this drawer carries no markings of a saw or plane. Much of the surface carries grooves that follow the grain of the wood, giving strong evidence that the board was reduced to its 5/8-inch thickness by riving. Circa 1800.

BOLINGER~

FIGURE 2–12
RIVING A BOARD

Riving was the process used to split a log into boards by driving a froe into the end of the log and opening it up along the natural run of the grain.

Plate 2–4). In contrast, the signature of the modern band saw, which replaced the pit saw, will have straight, evenly spaced saw kerfs (see Plate 2–5).

Once the board was sawed, it was smoothed with a hand plane. If the surface was to be exposed, it was smoothed further with a scraper. Since smoothing the board was a difficult task,

FIGURE 2–13
USING A PIT SAW

The tiller working from the top guided the saw to ensure that uniform boards were cut. The angle of the saw would naturally vary and the progress of the cutting would not be uniform; thus the signature of the pit saw will show off-angle kerfs unevenly spaced.

PLATE 2–4
SIGNATURE OF A PIT SAW
The uneven kerf widths and varying angle is a common feature of the pit saw.

PLATE 2–5

MODERN BAND SAW
SIGNATURE

The parallel saw kerfs indicate that the wood rested on a support that was uniformly positioned with respect to the blade, and the even spacing of the kerfs indicates that the wood was fed into the blade at a steady rate. These two features are not likely to be produced by a pit saw. Circa 1920.

unexposed surfaces were often left with the saw mark showing, or they were planed only enough to remove warp or to obtain the proper thickness. To determine where a surface was dressed with a hand plane, move your hand across the grain of an exposed area. You should feel an ever-so-slight irregularity in the surface. As you move your hand across the grain of an unexposed area,

PLATE 2–6

SIGNATURE OF THE ROUND-NOSE HAND PLANE

The work shown is the rear rail of a chest, and would not be seen. Therefore no effort was made to smooth the board any more than necessary.

you should feel a more definite pattern of ridges (Plate 2–6).

The earliest boring tool was the pod auger. Holes made with a pod auger have a slightly rounded bottom with no hole in the center. Holes drilled with a screw auger have a flat bottom with a small hole in the center, which is created by the lead screw. Early screw augers had a single spiral, whereas modern augers have a dual spiral (Figure 2–14).

Rotating Cutting

Any part of a piece of furniture that shows the signature of a rotating tool indicates either that the part is a replacement or that the entire work is relatively new. A surfacer or jointer used with a fast feed will create a ripple pattern across the grain of the stock (Plate 2–7). Molding formed by rotating routers will have a ripple across its face. Molding formed by a hand molding plane, on the other hand, will have imperfections across the contour of the molded surface (Figure 2–15).

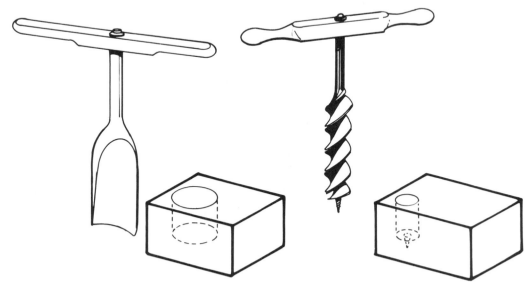

FIGURE 2–14

EARLY BORING TOOLS

The pod auger on the left is one of the oldest tools used for boring holes. The single-spiral screw auger appeared next and was the forerunner of modern boring devices.

PLATE 2–7
MODERN JOINTER
SIGNATURE

The ripple across the grain is the result of moving the stock too fast into the rotating cutting heads. The small ridge parallel to the grain and near the center of the board is caused by a chip in the cutter blades. Modern.

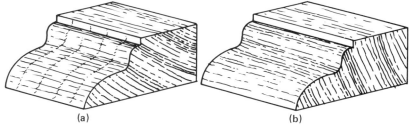

(a)   (b)

FIGURE 2–15a
SIGNATURE OF A MODERN ROUTER

Moldings made with a rotating router bit will show ripples running perpendicular to the face of the mold.

FIGURE 2–15b
SIGNATURE OF A MOLDING PLANE

Moldings made with a hand molding plane will have imperfections running parallel with the face of the mold.

Fasteners

Nails

It is difficult for us to realize the amount of work that went into the making of early nails. The earliest were made in England from "nail rods." These rods were made from Swedish and Russian steel. The craftsman would cut the rods to the desired length, and then hammer out the desired shape on a forge. These nails were not uniform in shape or size. Some had a hook rather than a head on the end. A later technique developed whereby after forming the body of the nail, the craftsman would clasp the nail in a pair of tongues and flatten one end to form the head. This hammered head is referred to as a rosebud head.

By 1750 the production of iron in America became so extensive that the English Parliament passed the Iron Act to prohibit the manufacturing of iron objects in America. Nevertheless, the colonists did take sheet iron and forge nails and other objects. Plate 2–8a shows examples of early

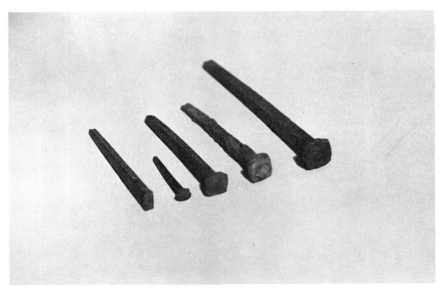

PLATE 2–8a

EXAMPLE OF EARLY NAILS

The two nails on the right are examples of early forged nails. The third and fourth nails from the right are early cut nails. The nail on the left is a modern flooring nail.

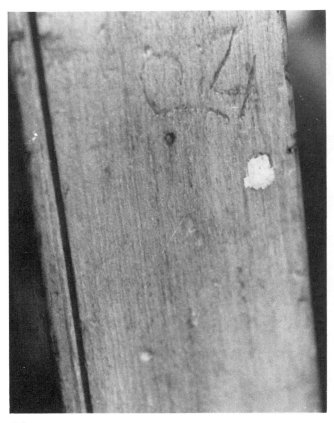

PLATE 2–8b

COVERED NAIL HEADS

Furniture that was originally painted or deeply stained had the nail heads concealed with a chalky substance. Once the original finish is lost, these nail holes become rather obvious. Even though they are not attractive, they should not be disturbed, if at all possible.

(b)

nails. The two nails on the right are forged nails. They were beaten out on an anvil. These are the earliest of the nails shown. This process was slow and laborious, making nails very precious. About 1780 the first nail-cutting machine was put to use. This machine produced nails that were uniform in size and shape. The third and fourth nails from the right are early cut nails. The nail on the left is a modern cut nail. This nail is used to put down tongue-and-groove hardwood flooring. Considering what we know about the manufacture of nails, square-cut nails can be expected in pieces of furniture constructed as early as 1790. The strap hinges shown in Plate 2–25 are secured with hand-forged nails. This feature makes it conceivable that this chest was constructed prior to 1790.

The square nail was a common fastener in country furniture, and the maker did not try to conceal the nail. Over the years the exposed head took on a patina that cannot be duplicated. In time, people began to paint the furniture to provide some color to their homes. When this was done, the nails were set below the surface of the wood and covered with plaster. This process completely concealed the nails.

Even though the nails found in a piece of furniture can indicate its age, it must be realized that early nails can be "planted" in more recently made furniture. When using nails as an indicator of age, other features should be considered.

Screws

About 1725 the first handmade screws were introduced. These were in great demand for fastening the hinges of drop-leaf tables. Early screws were quite crude. There was inaccuracy in the threads, the heads were slotted unevenly and frequently off center, and the ends were blunt. The process of making screws by hand was laborious, making the early screw very expensive. Because of the expense, screws were used sparingly in early furniture. It was not until 1850 that the screw-making machine became widely used. With early furniture, expect to see screws used only to secure hinges or other hardware. Furniture made after 1850 will have screws uniform in size and shape with sharp ends.

Hardware

Early hinges and latches were either cast brass or cast iron, the brass being reserved for the classical and expensive pieces. The British embargo of 1807–1815 caused a shortage of many manufactured items, including brass hardware. Thus the American craftsman became more dependent on local resources, and before long the American blacksmith became adept at designing and hammering out excellent strap iron hinges. Latches were made from wood turnbuckles and knobs (Figure 2–16). By 1840, the United States had a thriving brass and iron industry and could produce hardware as it was needed.

Now that we have discussed various parts, it would be useful to see what we might expect to find in an entire piece. Figure 2–17 illustrates the construction that might be found in an early table.

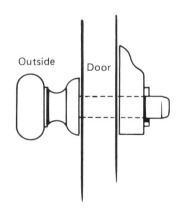

FIGURE 2–16
WOOD TURNBUCKLE

The country cabinetmaker's answer to brass or cast iron latches. This is a prized feature of country work, and an old one will show considerable wear where the latch has rubbed the surface.

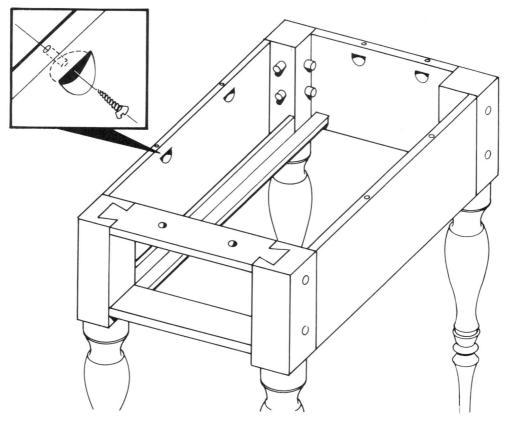

FIGURE 2–17
COMPOSITE VIEW OF EARLY TABLE CONSTRUCTION

An early table that has pinned mortise-and-tenon joints will usually show whittled pegs protruding through the inside face of the legs. There will be several gouged-out recesses on the inside face of the rails through which screws are inserted to hold the top in place. On a primitive table, nails may go directly through the top into the rail. The lower drawer divider will probably be secured with a mortise and tenon, while the upper divider will be secured to the leg by means of an open dovetail, as illustrated. The drawer guide and support will be secured to the inside of the end rails by either square nails or pegs. A table with well-turned legs and flush construction will most likely have a dovetailed drawer. Expect to be able to feel plane marks on the inside face of the rails, and check the legs for slight differences. Also note whether they are out of round. The rails and the legs should be made from single boards. Not until the twentieth century did it become common practice to face glue boards to secure needed thickness for such items as bed posts and table legs.

Bedsteads

Owing to their history and construction, bedsteads stand apart from other pieces of furniture and thus need to be discussed separately. Early sleeping accommodations were simply mats placed on the floor, and as late as the nineteenth century many poor people had never slept on a raised bed. Early bedsteads consisted of simple frames, often attached to two walls in the corner of a room, and they had only one post. Bedsteads for the well-to-do were usually recesses built into the wall.

In the eighteenth century bedsteads were made with tall posts so that a curtain could be hung around the bed for warmth. This type of bedstead eventually became known as a four-poster. Less elaborate bedsteads of that same period were made with short posts that barely

PLATE 2–9

TECHNIQUES FOR SECURING BED RAILS

The item in the foreground is the bottom of a post from a bedstead made around 1890–1900. The cast iron lock plate set flush into the post has two slots that receive the tabs on a second cast iron piece secured to the bed rail. The tabs would be inserted at the top of the slots, and when they dropped down under the weight of the rail, they would be tightly wedged in place. The second item is the rail end from a bed made around 1870. The heavy cast iron hook fits into a groove cut into the bedpost, where it hooks over a pin that had been positioned across the groove. The third item is the end of a rail of a rope bed. It is secured to the post, and is held secure with the long iron bolt. The plug seen in the side was used to cover the hole drilled for the threaded piece of iron with which the bolt would engage (circa 1860). The fourth item is the rail of a rope bed with threads on the end that allow it to be screwed into the bedpost (circa 1850). The rail in the background seems characteristic of an early rope bed, but the blocks attached to the top indicate that it belongs to an early slat bed. The dowel on the end of the rail fits into a hole in the bedpost and is held secure with a small pin. It is difficult to date this work. It may have been done around 1850–1870. The bedding for this bedstead was probably a tick of corn shucks or straw.

extended above the frame where the bedding was placed. Such beds have come to be known as hired-hands' beds.

The age of a bedstead can be determined from the technique by which the side rails were fastened to the post. Early free-standing bedsteads were usually secured with a pinned mortise and tenon. Since bedsteads needed to be taken apart for moving, the mortise and tenon were held together with a long bolt that passed through the post and screwed into a threaded piece of metal in the rail. Still another type of bedstead was the rope bedstead, which was so named because ropes were stretched across the frame to support the bedding. It was constructed either with a mortise and tenon or an iron bolt,

or in some cases had wood threads present on the end of the rails that allowed the rails to be screwed into the post. These threads are made in such a way that weight on the bed causes the rails to twist and tighten the threads. This is possible because one end of each rail has a left-hand thread and one end has a right-hand thread.

By the Victorian period, iron devices came into use as a means of holding rails to the post. The early devices were heavy cast iron. More recent bedsteads from around the 1930s use thin double-hook metal devices on the rail ends that fit into slots cut into the post; these devices hook over metal pins in the post. (Plate 2–9 shows various techniques for assembling a bedstead.)

Typical Features of Old Work

Plates 2–1 and 2–32 illustrate features to look for when you are examining a piece of furniture to determine its age. Not all such features are shown, but the ones here should at least answer some preliminary questions about the age of an item. Expect to see several of these features in a piece of furniture, and be suspicious of any work that has only one or two features that hint at its age.

If a step cupboard has square nails but no worn corners or nicks, or shows the signature of a modern planer, for example, be doubtful of its age. Regardless of how many features on a piece of furniture attest to its age, if there is a large sum of money involved, get a second opinion.

It is not possible to illustrate every conceivable feature here, but if the features presented are used as a basic guide, the reader should, with a little experience, be able to judge the age of a piece of furniture.

PLATE 2–10a

DOVETAIL CONSTRUCTION IN A DRAWER

This is the typical style of a handmade dovetail joint in a drawer. Notice that the dovetails are much wider than the pins. The scribe line is a distinctive feature to look for as it indicates that the drawer was layed out by hand. The bottom of the drawer shows a bevel for fitting the drawer into the grooves in the front and the sides. The light-colored divider area on the bottom indicates that the bottom has rubbed on the drawer divider with the wearing away of the drawer sides. This drawer was made in the middle 1800's.

PLATE 2–10b

Close-up of the drawer to show a typical example of scribe marks and saw kerfs.

PLATE 2–11
DRAWER CONSTRUCTION

This drawer shows evidence of being planed with a round-nose plane. The hand beveled edges are an excellent feature. The gnaw marks made by a rat should be left as is. The drawer bottom is secured to the back of the drawer with three small square nails. Circa 1850–1860.

(a)

(b)

PLATE 2–12a,b
PIN CONSTRUCTION

The extended pin technique was used for a brief period of time in drawer construction. Needless to say, it is a machine operation. The machine used to cut dovetails was introduced shortly afterwards and this technique soon disappeared. Circa 1900.

PLATE–2–13
MACHINE DOVETAILS

Machine-made dovetails have pins and dovetails of equal size. Notice the lack of scribe marks. Modern.

PLATE 2–14
EARLY DRAWER CONSTRUCTION

This drawer has two significant features. It has through dovetails at the rear corner, and the bottom slides under the back. Since the drawer bottom bears no signature of a saw or plane, it was probably reduced to size by riving. This drawer was constructed around 1800.

PLATE 2–15
WEAR POINTS

This is a close-up of the left door of the cupboard shown in Plate 6–15. The indention in the edge of the door is unquestionably a sign that the door was repeatedly opened by the fingernails. Such wear should never be repaired. Also notice the through mortise-and-tenon construction on the door.

PLATE 2–16
RODENT DAMAGE

This is a close-up of the bottom of the same door shown in plate 2–15. The hole was caused by a mouse or rat and should be left as is.

PLATE 2–17
EARLY CARVING

This foot on the American Empire desk shown in Plate 6–1 is a good example of deep carving. Since it is not identical to the companion foot on the other post, it was probably carved by hand. The small chips in the column and the rounded corners on the block immediately above the foot are signs of age.

PLATE 2–18

This carving is at the top of the post that ends in the foot shown in Plate 2–17. Once again, notice the depth of the cuts. The hair line fractures in the veneer, the wear around the lid support, and the subtle dents in the brass pull are all signs of age.

PLATE 2–19
LATER CARVING

The example of carving shown here gives evidence of the decline in artistry in the twentieth century. In general the design is well laid out, but the cuts are not deep. The legs end in a claw-and-ball foot that is reasonably well done. One detrimental feature is that the leg terminates at the base of the cabinet rather than extended upward and forming a corner post. This piece was probably made around 1920–1930.

PLATE 2–20
PEGGED SLAT

The protrusion of the pin that was used to secure the slat to the chair post indicates that the post was made from unseasoned wood. This assumption is further supported by the fact that the turned post is out of round. (When unseasoned wood is turned on a lathe, it is originally round, but with time the turn will shrink across the grain.) Circa 1800.

PLATE 2–21
GATELEG TABLE

These plates illustrate important features of the construction of a gateleg table. Notice the scribe marks made when the hinge for the gateleg rail was constructed. Also note the manner in which the gateleg is notched so it can fit in line with the stationary legs when the table is closed. The pin holding the hinge may be made of either wood or iron. This table was constructed in southern Indiana. Circa 1850.

PLATE 2–22
SINGLE-BOARD CONSTRUCTION

The rear view of the chest featured in Chapter 4 reveals single-board construction with upper and lower rails, secured with pinned mortise and tenons. These features are signs of age. Generally speaking, the more numerous and smaller the panels, the newer the work. The board shown here is poplar and is 28 inches wide.

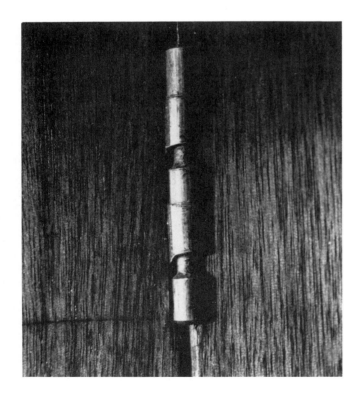

PLATE 2–23
HARDWARE

This hinge is on the step cupboard featured in Plate 6–8. The hinges on this piece were so badly worn that the doors had to be lifted vertically before they could close. Rather than discard hinges of this age and condition, however, turn them over, as has been done for the hinge above. Now the weight of the door bears on the other edge of the knuckle and can provide another 140 years of opening and closing.

PLATE 2–24
STRAP IRON HINGES

Hinges of this type were commonly used on six-board, dovetailed blanket chests of the 1800's. The hinge is secured with early handmade screws.

PLATE 2–25
STRAP IRON HINGES

The overlap of the knuckle strap indicates that these hinges are handmade. The hinges are attached to the immigrant chest with very crude handmade nails. Circa prior to 1790.

PLATE 2–26
HANDMADE HINGES

This set of handmade hinges was taken from a drop leaf table that was beyond repair. Notice the overlap of the knuckle strip. The table from which these hinges were taken was cherry. The legs and rails were painted deep blue. The table was eaten by worms, and its loss was much regretted.

(a)

(b)

PLATE 2–27
DROP LEAF JOINTS

(a) From a table made in 1957. (b) From a table made in the early 1800's. The older joint is less pronounced and the roll is not a perfect quarter-round.

PLATE 2–28
EARLY TURNED DRAWER PULLS

In contrast to the typical drawer pulls of 1850, these knobs have the grain of the stock running parallel with the axis of the knobs. This indicates that the lathe did not have face-plate capabilities and the knobs had to be turned in the way a spindle is turned. This type of knob is rarer than the cross-grain or discturned knob.

PLATE 2–29
DRAWER GUIDES

If the work being inspected includes a drawer, remove the drawer and inspect the drawer guides. If they have not been replaced, expect to see a groove worn in the drawer runner. On an old piece the drawer runner will be secured with square nails or wood pegs. Plate 2–29 shows the inside of a chest of drawers. Notice the hand planed level on the end panel, and the scribe marks where the mortise joint was located for the top end rail. The wear on the drawer runner extends half the width of the runner stock.

PLATE 2–30
CHAIR WEAR

The age of a chair can often be determined by observing the extent of wear on the front round, where people tend to put their feet.

PLATE 2–31
WEAR ON A CHILD'S CHAIR

Notice the flat area on the front post of this child's chair. As the child began to learn to walk the chair was turned over on its front or back, and the child, using it for support, would slide it across the floor. Occasionally a child's high chair might be cut down once the child outgrew the need for it. Chairs of this type were often made of maple or ash, and the slats were usually pinned into mortises cut in the rear posts.

PLATE 2–32
EARLY CHIPPENDALE LOCK ESCUTCHEON, CIRCA 1790

This fine example of early hardware is mounted on an early chest. It has a superb dull luster finish that can come only with age. Slight irregularities and slightly chamfered edges indicate that the hardware was formed by hand.

3

Repair Concepts

Since there is no reasonable way to illustrate every conceivable type of damage that can come to a piece of furniture, perhaps the best way to discuss repair concepts is to define categories of damage that cover most situations. Over the years I have found that the following types of damage recur consistently:

1. Lost width
2. Lost length
3. Fractured parts
4. Damaged areas

This list may not cover every situation, but it certainly includes the most common restoration problems. It should be kept in mind that these categories were developed with the idea of preserving as much of the original work as possible. Certainly in many cases it would be simpler to replace the damaged portion of the work. When this is done, however, the antique value of the work is greatly reduced.

Restoring Lost Width

Restoring lost width is probably the simplest form of repair. If part of a top is missing, the restoration is simply a matter of securing wood of the same kind and age, truing the edges, and gluing the needed width onto the original piece. If the missing portion bore some type of design or carving, the procedure becomes slightly more involved.

The need to restore width probably arises most often in the case of drawer sides. These items withstand tremendous wear, but in time they wear down to the groove that holds the bottom in place, and eventually they split. When worn sides cause drawers to stick, even more damage can occur, as we will see later. When repairing drawer sides, try not to disturb the joints that hold the drawer sides to the back and front. Although this is not always possible, it can be done if the wear has not gone into the groove for the bottom. Once the wear has spread into this goove, it is best to take the drawer apart.

Let's take the worst case first. Carefully disassemble the drawer and, with a hand plane or table saw, true the damaged edge of the drawer sides. Next, glue an extender piece of sufficient width onto the original side (Figure 3–1a). After the glue has dried, you can remove the excess thickness and length, but do not remove the excess width at this time. Using the undamaged dovetails and pins as guides, align the drawer front and drawer side. With the dovetail on the drawer front serving as a pattern, scribe the outline for the missing pins on the added width extender (Figure 3–1b). When the joint has been cut out and the proper fit has been made, locate the position of and cut the groove for the bottom in the side (Figure 3–1c). Assemble the drawer without glue, and using a framing square, strike a line along the side that is at a 90-degree angle to the drawer front and is located at a point that is even with the bottom edge of the drawer front (Figure 3–1d).

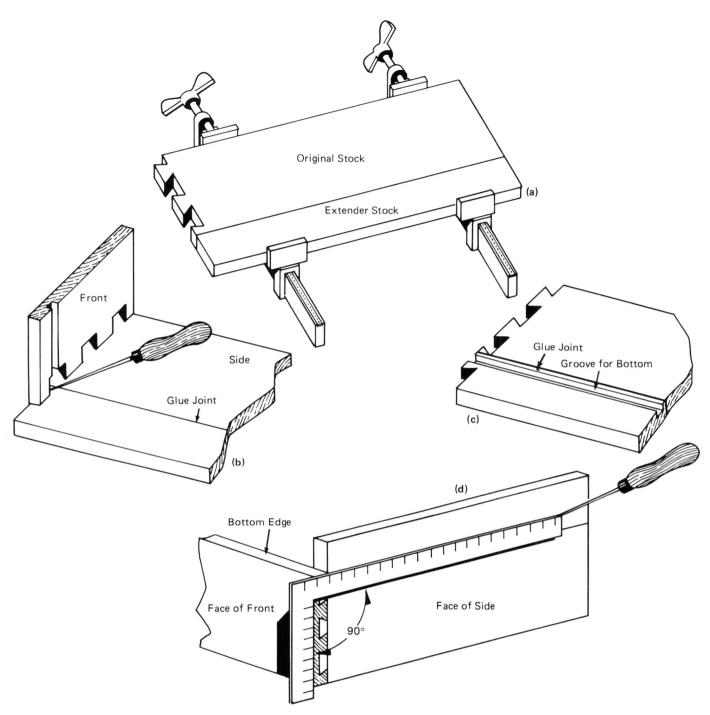

FIGURE 3–1a

The extender stock should be of the same kind of wood. It can be glued in place and dressed to the proper thickness and length. Extra width should not be removed until the drawer is about to be reassembled.

FIGURE 3–1b

Align the original joints that still exist on the front and side to the extent possible and scribe the outlines of the dovetail on the drawer front onto the drawer side. Also mark the area where the groove for the bottom is to be cut.

FIGURE 3–1c

Cut the new pins in the extender piece, as well as the groove for the bottom.

FIGURE 3–1d

Assemble the drawer front and side without glue. Scribe a line locating the correct width along the full length of the drawer side. Square the line off the face of the drawer front so that the drawer will fit properly in the chest.

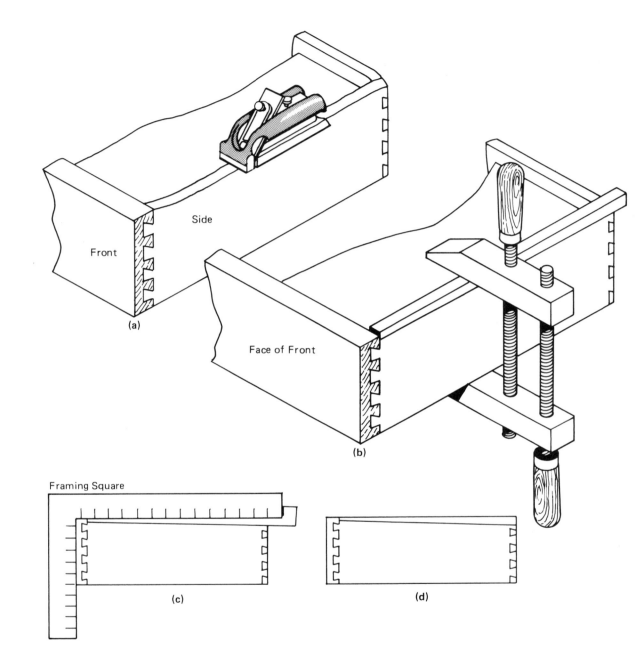

(a) Side / Front

(b) Face of Front

(c) Framing Square

(d)

FIGURE 3–2a

Carefully true the edge of the side. A rabbet plane works well here because the blade can be replaced at the front of the frame and thus the work can be planed in the corners.

FIGURE 3–2b

Glue an extender in place and allow it to dry. Do not worry about exact length or width at this time.

FIGURE 3–2c

Using the framing square and working with the drawer front as a reference, strike a line along the length of the extender stock. When the extender is planed to this line, the side will be square to the front of the drawer. The drawer should then fit into the chest properly.

FIGURE 3–2d

The drawer is now repaired and ready for use.

Disassemble the drawer, and plane the side down to the line. Now the drawer can be glued for the final assembly.

If the drawer side is not badly worn, but worn enough to prevent the drawer from opening easily, do not take the drawer apart. Instead, use a rabbet plane carefully to dress the edge of the side to the point where it is square to the face of the side (Figure 3–2a). The edge does not have to be perfectly straight because the extender stock is usually thin enough to bend to fit the contour of the edge when clamped. Remember, the object is to preserve the original fit of the joints in the drawer. The next step is to glue on a strip wide enough to restore the side to an overall width in excess of the width of the drawer front (Figure 3–2b). When the glue is dry, use a framing square (working from the

bottom edge of the drawer front) to run a line off the face of the front along the full length of the drawer side. Using this line as a guide, remove the excess wood from the extender portion of the drawer (Figure 3–2c, d).

As a rule, a drawer that opens and closes with ease should not be repaired even though the sides show considerable wear. However, there is one exception. You will notice when working with furniture that has veneer on the drawer dividers that the veneer may have considerable damage where the drawer has been dragged across the divider (Figure 3–3a). If the veneer is repaired and the drawer is left unrepaired, the veneer will simply become damaged again.

Two other things can be done to prevent further damage. First, the drawer guide and run-

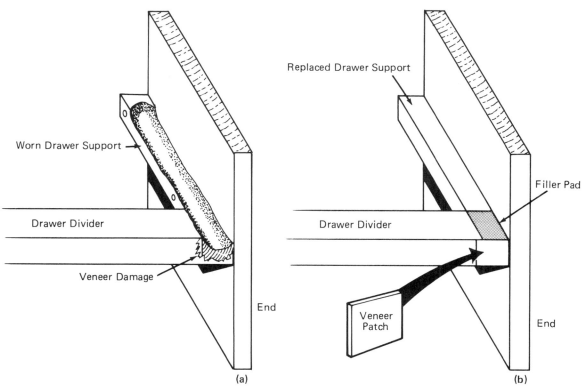

(a)   (b)

FIGURE 3–3a

The worn drawer support has allowed the drawer to ride excessively on the drawer divider and has cut a groove across the divider. The veneer on the divider has been chipped away at this point.

FIGURE 3–3b

To prevent further damage to the veneer, replace the drawer support and glue a filler pad of wood in the groove worn into the drawer divider. Once this is done, the veneer can be repaired.

ner should be repaired. Second, a pad should be placed in the worn groove formed across the divider by the drawer side (Figure 3–3b). The pad will hold the drawer off the veneer and prevent it from chipping in the future.

Restoring Lost Length

Restoring lost length is somewhat more complex in that the wood fibers of two pieces must be parallel if gluing is to be successful. Since no parallel alignment occurs when end grain is placed to end grain, some type of joint must be designed to provide the parallel feature. If the stock being extended in length is a square or a round, such as a table leg or chair leg, the dowel-and-hole technique can be used. Basically, this technique involves four steps:

1. True the end of the damaged piece.
2. Bore a hole, on center, into the original stock.
3. Fit the dowel on the length extender into the hold and glue in place.
4. Shape the extender to match the size and contour of the original stock.

With the dowel inserted into the hole, the wood fibers will be parallel and a strong joint ensured (Figure 3–4).

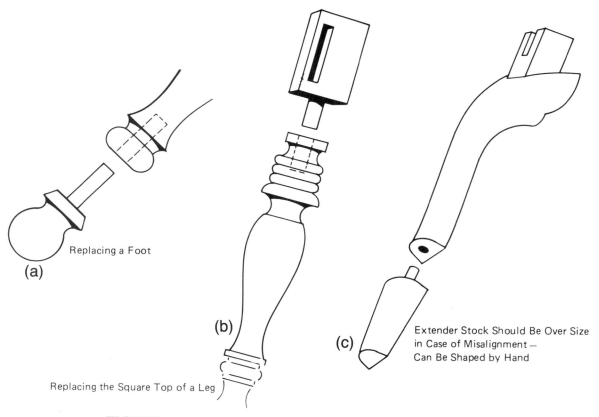

Replacing a Foot

(a)

(b)

Replacing the Square Top of a Leg

(c)

Extender Stock Should Be Over Size in Case of Misalignment — Can Be Shaped by Hand

FIGURE 3–4

If possible, make the dowel on the extender at least 1 inch in diameter. In some cases the design can be used to conceal the repair (a,c). If it cannot, make the extender oversized so that it can be worked down to match the profile of the original stock after the parts have been assembled (c).

Should an extension have to be made for a flat board similar to a cupboard with a solid end having a foot cut into the board, you will find that the lap joint works well here. The first step is to remove the damaged part of the work (see Figure 3–5a). Working from the inside to conceal the repair, cut a large lap joint on the face of the original board. Next, make an extender of adequate width and length and cut a matched lap joint on it (Figure 3–5b). The extender is then glued in place. Using the length of the front leg as a guide, and squaring from the front edge of the end, mark the correct length of the extender. The portion of the pattern that was lost is now drawn on the extender and the proper shape cut (Figure 3–5c).

As mentioned earlier, worn drawers tend to stick and thus can damage a piece of furniture. For example, the pins on the dovetail joint of a drawer front can be broken as shown in Figure 3–6a. Drawer fronts are a vital part of a piece of furniture, and the loss of one can reduce the

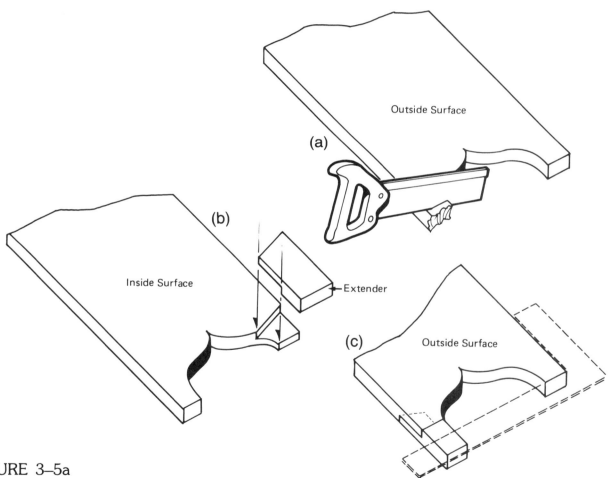

FIGURE 3–5a

Remove the damaged portion of the foot.

FIGURE 3–5b

On the inside surface cut a half lap joint as large as is feasible. Also cut a matching half lap joint on the extender stock.

FIGURE 3–5c

Glue the extender in place, redraw the original pattern, and shape the extender stock according to the pattern. The placement of the framing square illustrates how to determine the correct length of the extender in relation to the full length of the front foot.

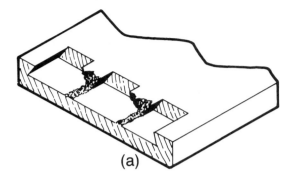

(a)

FIGURE 3–6a

The narrow pins have been broken.

FIGURE 3–6b

Slots are cut back into the drawer front on the inside surface, and located where the pins were originally situated.

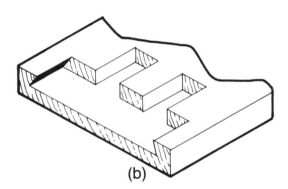

(b)

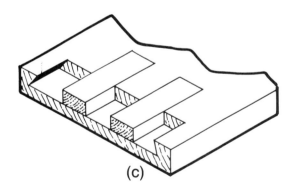

(c)

FIGURE 3–6c

Glue extender stock into these slots, allowing the stock to extend to the end of the drawer front.

FIGURE 3–6d

Even though the pins have already been proved to be too thin, reshape the extender stock to the original size and shape so that the drawer side will remain unchanged.

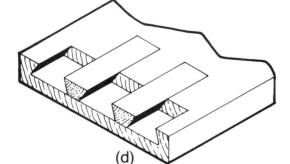

(d)

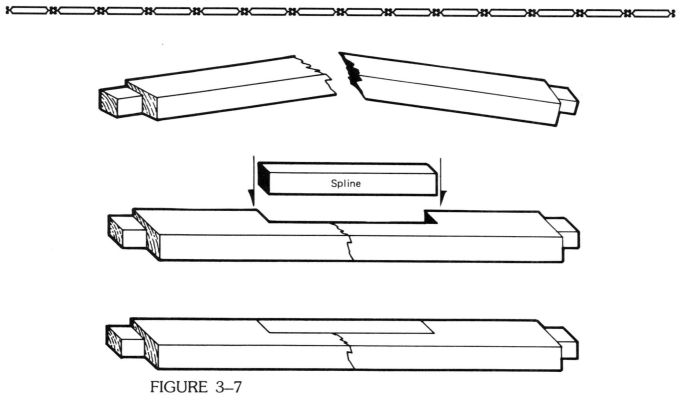

FIGURE 3–7

As a first step, the broken drawer divider may be reglued at the fracture in order to regain the correct position. However, a spline will then have to be used to strengthen the original stock.

value of the work. To salvage a drawer front damaged in this way and to conceal the repair, cut back into the drawer front from the inside face as shown in Figure 3–6b. These slots are cut in the exact location of the pins. Extender blocks are then fitted into these slots to form a type of lap joint (Figure 3–6c). Using the drawer side as a pattern, shape the blocks to match the original pins (Figure 3–6d).

Strengthening Fractured Parts

Ill-fitting drawers can also cause the drawer dividers to break, as illustrated in Figure 3–7. To repair such damage you will have to bring the two pieces together just as they were originally. From the back edge, cut out a notch to receive a spline. The spline can then be glued in place and dressed down to whatever size is needed. Figure 3–7 depicts a break that is directly across the grain. If such a split should happen to run down the grain rather than across, the pieces can be reglued without a spline by making use of the parallel alignment of the grain.

A common problem in pieces constructed of bentwood, of which the Windsor chair is an excellent example, is that the wood tends to split along the grain. It is extremely difficult to draw the split within a curve back into the proper radius and glue the wood in place. Therefore, some type of splint must be designed to repair the fracture and restore the original strength. This form of repair is necessary here because the strength of bentwood construction depends on the counter pressures created by the overall

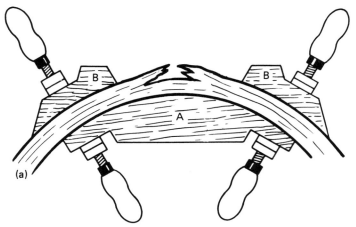

FIGURE 3–8a

The inside support block (A) bridges the weak portion of the bentwood, and the outside support blocks (B) provide the support needed to maintain the curve of the stock while repairs are being made. These blocks should be firmly clamped in place, as shown, during the entire repair process.

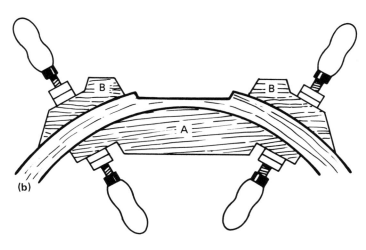

FIGURE 3–8b

With the support blocks in place, cut away the damaged portion of the stock. Notice the taper of the cut.

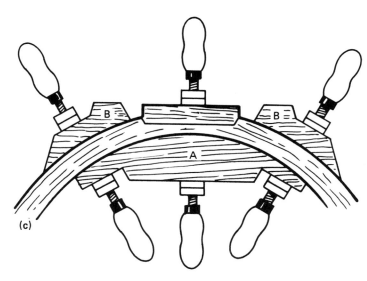

FIGURE 3–8c

A block is glued in place and allowed to dry. The repair block should be flaired as shown to help prevent the outer fibers from splitting further. The clamps and support blocks can now be removed and the repair block can be carefully worked down to match the contour of the original work.

stress of the bends. Equally important, the bend on either side of the fracture must be maintained while the split is being repaired (see Figure 3–8).

Covering Damaged Areas

Damaged areas can usually be covered with a plug. Begin by cutting the plug and tapering the edges just slightly. Hold the plug over the damaged area, and with the under cut of the taper facing down, scribe an outline of the plug. Be sure that the grain of the plug runs in the same direction as the grain of the work being repaired. Cut out the damaged portion of the surface, staying inside the scribe lines. After a trial fit, glue the plug in place using a clamp to force the plug into the hole and letting the tapered edges form a wedge (Figure 3–9).

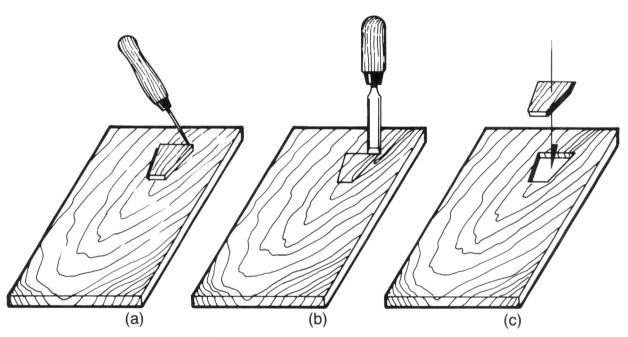

(a)   (b)   (c)

FIGURE 3–9a

Scribe an outline of the plug onto the damaged surface.

FIGURE 3–9b

Using a chisel and mallet, cut the cross-grain scribe lines first, then the scribe lines that run parallel with the grain of wood.

FIGURE 3–9c

Remove the wood within the scribe lines, fit the plug in place with glue, and then level it out.

4

Fixing the Broken

In this chapter we illustrate how the basic concept and techniques of restoration have actually been applied. The ultimate goal of all the work illustrated here has been to preserve as much of the original piece as possible.

Restoring an Early Rocker

The rocking chair shown in Plate 4–1 is a fine example of an early chair that merits restoration. The chair is unusual in that it has the original seat. Thus the entire restoration process must be geared to preserving the seat. The antique value of the chair would be greatly reduced if the original seat were removed.

Plate 4–2 illustrates some of the damage that has come to the chair. The support round on the left side of the seat has come out of the leg, and the splintered portion has long been lost. In addition, the right arm has a split caused by a square-headed nail used to secure the arm to the post (Plate 4–3). The split is very old and cannot be closed. There will be no attempt to repair this damage in that it attests to the age of the work.

The first step in repairing the post was to smooth the damaged area and to form a flat surface onto which a repair block could be glued. During this time the seat was covered with cloth soaked with a mixture of water and fabric soft-

PLATE 4–1

The exact age of the rocking chair is unknown. Its overall features place it in the 1800's. The rockers resemble those on Connecticut short-arm rockers. (Courtesy of Shaker Table Antiques)

PLATE 4–3

The right arm carries a very old split caused by an earlier attempt at repair. This split attests to the age of the work.

PLATE 4–2

Weight on the seat has caused the left seat support to split out of the side of the front post. The splintered portion of the post is lost.

ener so as to make the seat material less brittle and reduce the possibility of damage to the seat. A clamp was used to pull the seat support gradually back to its original position. This work was

done over a period of 12 hours, during which time the seat was kept wet and the clamp tightened every two hours. Plate 4–4 shows the position of the seat support at the end of the 12 hours.

The seat became sufficiently stretched to allow the clamp to be removed momentarily so

PLATE 4–4

The seat support was gradually pulled back into place over a twelve-hour period. The seat was kept wet during the entire process.

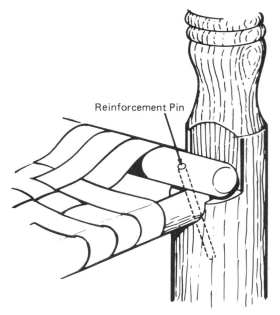

Reinforcement Pin

FIGURE 4–1

A small rod is used to reinforce the joint.

PLATE 4–5

The seat support has been secured to its proper place and the prepared replacement piece is ready to be glued in place.

PLATE 4–6

The replacement block has now been glued tightly in place.

that glue could be added to the joint where the seat support belonged. The clamp was then applied once again and kept in place (to hold the seat support firmly to the leg) until the glue was dry. A ⅛-inch steel rod was placed in the leg to reinforce the joint (Figure 4–1).

While the glue was drying, a replacement piece was fashioned to fit the damaged area. Plate 4–5 shows the replacement piece as it is being readied for gluing. Plate 4–6 shows the piece glued in place and drying. Once the glue had set, the repair piece was shaped with a hand file, chisel, and sandpaper. As a final step, color was added to blend the repair work into the original work (Plates 4–7 and 4–8).

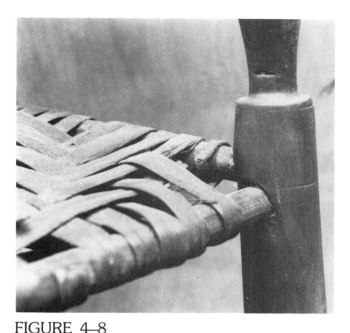

FIGURE 4–8

The block has been shaped, the original scribe lines have been carried over into the replacement piece, and color has been added to blend the repair into the original work.

PLATE 4–7

The shaping of the block to the contour of the leg is almost complete.

Preserving a Single-Board Top

The top shown in Plate 4–9 is from a six-board blanket chest. The split is very old and has remained unrepaired for so long that the splintered edge has shrunk. Glue in the wood indicates that an earlier unsuccessful attempt has been made to repair the top. Since new glue will not bond to old glue, the first task here was to clean the edge. In the process of cleaning, great care was taken not to alter the contours of the split. The edges were cleaned with a circular wire brush attached to an electric hand drill. The bristles were stiff enough to remove the glue, but not so stiff as to damage the wood fiber (Plate 4–10).

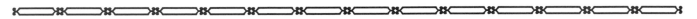

PLATE 4–9

The top of a blanket chest with a split that was left unrepaired for several years. As a result, the wood along the split edge has shrunk.

Plate 4–11 shows that the top had a severe bow. This bow had to be maintained during the gluing to ensure that the edges being glued matched. The clamp on top of the board provided counterpressure for the clamps on the bottom. This in turn placed sufficient pressure on the joint. Once dry, the top was placed in the sun, bowed side up, and after a few hours the board became perfectly flat (Plate 4–12).

PLATE 4–10

All old glue and dirt must be cleaned from the split edges without damaging the wood fiber.

FIGURE 4–11

The board must be reglued with the bow present. The counter pressure of the clamps make it possible to place enough force on the edges for the glue to be effective.

To prevent the bow from returning to the board, a heavy coat of sealer was applied to keep out moisture. A split of this magnitude and age cannot be closed perfectly. However, the grain of the wood on either side of the split should make it obvious to any observer that this top was made from a single board—a fact that enhances the value of the chest.

PLATE 4–12

After lying in the sun with the bowed side up, the top is once again flat, and the crack is closed as well as can be expected for damage so old.

Repairing a Table Leg

The table leg shown in Plate 4–13 is that of a walnut kitchen table. This type of break is not uncommon, as it occurs at a weak point created by the turn. The flat object behind the leg is a piece of strap iron used as a support in an earlier attempt to repair the leg.

Although the leg could have been repaired without removing it from the frame, it was removed for convenience. This was done by tapping on the inside of the leg very gently until the mortise-and-tenon joint broke free. Next, the damaged part was sawed off at a natural break in the design, but an effort was made to keep as much of the original stock as possible. The damaged portion was removed at the lower edge of the bead and at the small shoulder where the leg returns to its full diameter (Plates 4–14 and 4–15).

The center of the leg on the upper and lower portions was then located as shown in Plate 4–16, so that a hole could be drilled in the center of the stock. The hole was drilled with the aid of a lathe (Plate 4–17). A 1-inch bit was placed in the head stock, and the leg was centered off the tail stock. The bit was aligned with the scribed center to ensure that a perfectly straight hole

PLATE 4–13

Walnut Kitchen Table. (Courtesy Seabury Antiques). It is not uncommon for a fracture like the one shown to occur at a weak point caused by the turning.

PLATE 4–14

The damaged portion of the leg is sawed out at a natural break in the design.

FIGURE 4–15

The upper portion of the damaged area is being cut out.

PLATE 4–16

A centering tool is used to locate the center of the top part of the original leg. The same procedure is carried out for the bottom portion of the leg.

PLATE 4–17

Taking advantage of the wood lathe to drill a perfectly true hole in the top portion of the leg.

PLATE 4–18

A simpler but less accurate way to bore holes into stock.

would be drilled. With the wood clamp holding the stock true, the lathe was turned on and the stock moved forward by turning the tail stock feed. This is a complicated procedure and great care should be taken with it. Plate 4–18 shows a simpler way of drilling the hole. Although this technique requires a good eye, with practice the craftsperson can learn to drill a true hole.

The next step was to turn the replacement stock. Plate 4–19 shows the replacement stock

PLATE 4–19

The completed replacement piece for the leg.

PLATE 4–20

The three parts of the leg ready for assembly.

after it was turned to the exact shape and length of the portion that had been cut out. Plate 4–20 shows the leg ready to be reassembled. The dowel portions of the extender and some glue were then placed in the appropriate holes, and the extender was clamped in place (Plate 4–21). Plates 4–22 and 4–23 show the repaired leg after the table was reassembled. When the old finish was removed from the table, some of the mixture was wiped over the replaced part in order to blend the old and new together. With the refinishing completed, the top was put in place, and the table was ready for its second 100 years of use.

PLATE 4–21

The replacement section glued and clamped in place.

A repair of this magnitude will not reduce the antique value of the table significantly. This procedure can be used to replace damaged feet on a leg or even the square top of a leg having damaged mortises that are fitted for rail tenons.

Restoring a Chest of Drawers

The chest of drawers shown in Plate 4–24 was found exposed to the weather under a roof and on a dirt floor. Despite its condition, it was found to have several redeeming features: it is solid cherry, handmade, has a single-board top, and is very old. Plates 4–25 to 4–30 illustrate the damage that had come to the chest.

PLATE 4–22

A close-up view of the restored leg. Notice that the replacement piece starts and ends at a natural break in the design.

PLATE 4–23

The reassembled table.

PLATE 4–24

A very early and fine handmade cherry chest.

PLATE 4–25

Damaged right front foot. This damage was caused by a combination of rot and termites.

PLATE 4–26a

Drawer with split drawer side.

PLATE 4–26b

Drawer with side and front damage. A nail is visible where an attempt was made to repair a split. That repair merely caused more damage.

PLATE 4–27

Single-board back (an important feature) carrying the signature of a round-nose hand plane has been split down the center.

PLATE 4–28

The rear feet have rotted from the post. Note that the tenons broken off from the rear rail are resting in the mortises in the post.

PLATE 4–29

Original location of the tenon can be seen, as well as wear due to opening and closing of the drawer. (The crack between the post and the end of the drawer divider caused by this broken tenon can be seen just under the drawer in Plate 4–26.)

PLATE 4–30

The end view of the broken tenons of the lower back rail. Notice the scribe lines that located these tenons are still present. Despite the severe damage, it is better to preserve this rail than try to replace it.

The chest was first taken apart. This was rather a simple task since it stayed together only long enough to be photographed (see Plate 4–24). During the restoration, some of the steps overlapped. That is to say, while a leg was under clamp waiting for the glue to dry, work on the frame was in progress.

Starting with the front foot, measurements were made and a replacement foot (with a dowel to fit up into the original stock) was turned. Plate 4–31 illustrates where the damaged left foot was to be removed. The cut was made at the point where the stock becomes square so that the repair

could be completely concealed. After the foot was removed, the center of the post was located (Plate 4–32). A hole 1 inch in diameter and approximately 3 inches deep was then bored into the post (Plate 4–33), and the replacement foot glued in place (Plate 4–34).

The next task is to repair the drawers. There exist two levels of damage on the drawers. The first shows typical damage to the sides of the drawer (Plate 4–26a). The drawer shown in Plate 4–26b reveals damage to the drawer front as well as to the sides. The drawer in Plate 4–26a will be considered first.

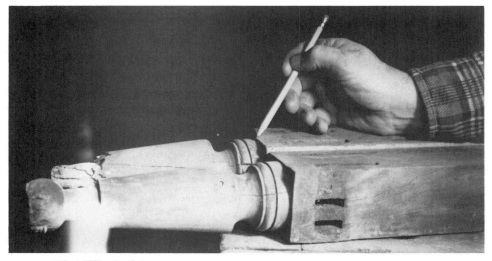

PLATE 4–31

Point at which the damaged foot will be removed. If the damaged part is cut off here, the repair will be completely hidden.

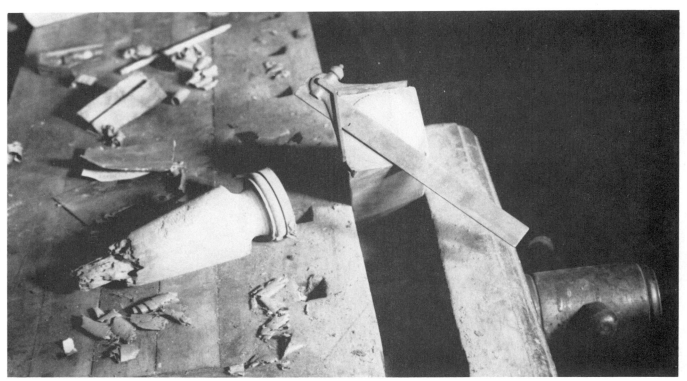

PLATE 4–32

Preparing the front post for drilling at the center.

PLATE 4–33

The hole has been drilled and is ready to receive the new foot, which has been turned.

Since about ½ an inch of the side is missing on the drawer shown in Plate 4–26a, it will be best to take the drawer apart, and true the edge of the remaining stock with a plane. This is shown in Plate 4–35. Once the edge has been trued, extra stock is glued onto the side to regain the lost width (Plate 4–36). The hand clamp shown prevents the pieces of wood from buckling under the pressure of the bar clamps.

After the glue has set, the front of the drawer is reassembled with the side, using the undamaged pins and dovetails as guides. The width needed for the side is marked, as is the pattern of the bottom dovetail. Plate 4–37 shows a craftsperson using a knife to mark the pattern of the dovetail. Once the drawer side is refitted to the drawer front, the position of the groove for the bottom is marked on the side, and cut (Plate 4–38). The groove for the bottom can be cut in the same manner, as explained in Chapter

PLATE 4–34

The new foot in place.

PLATE 4–35

Preparing the rough edge of a drawer side for the gluing of a width extender.

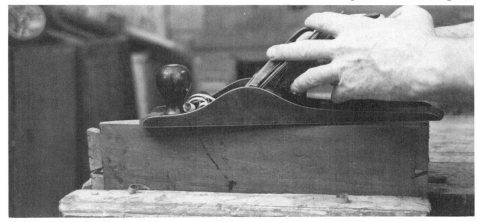

PLATE 4–36

Glueing the width extender in place.

PLATE 4–37

The craftsperson marks the correct width of the side, and transfers the pattern of the dovetail onto the repaired side.

PLATE 4–38

Locating the position of the groove for the bottom.

5, where drawer construction is discussed. Plates 4–39 and 4–40 show the drawer with all repairs completed. Compare Plate 4–26a to Plate 4–40.

Now let us look at the second drawer. I wanted to treat this drawer separately. Looking at the drawer in Plate 4–26b, some people might be tempted to replace the entire front. But this drawer front can be saved. As Plate 4–41 shows,

PLATE 4–39

Inside view of the repaired drawer.

PLATE 4–40

Repaired side refitted to the drawer front.

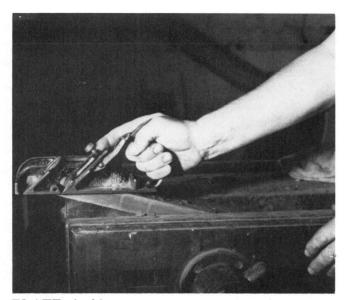

PLATE 4–41

The versatile rabbet plane is used to true up a damaged area.

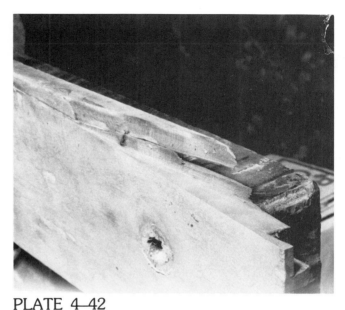

PLATE 4–42

The damaged area ready to receive the repair block. Notice the reglued split that is parallel to the bottom edge of the drawer front.

a rabbet plane is being used to form a wedge-shaped area where the damage exists (Plate 4–42). A repair piece can now be chosen that matches as closely as possible in color and grain, shaped in the form of a wedge. This is shown in Figure 4–2. Plate 4–43 shows the wedge clamped in place.

Once the glue has set, the excess length and thickness of the wedge can be removed. Then the damage to the drawer sides can be repaired as discussed earlier. Plate 4–44 shows the drawer after all the repairs have been completed. It looks quite different from that shown in Plate 4–26b.

FIGURE 4–2

Whenever a repair plug is wedge shaped, care must be taken to have the grain on the plug be parallel with the grain on the surface being repaired.

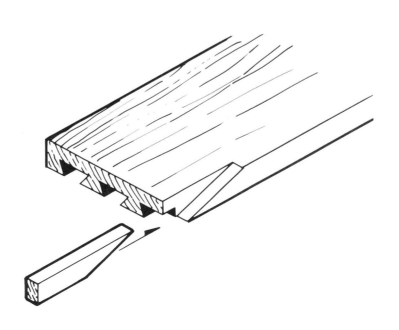

PLATE 4–43

The repair plug glued in place.

The rear legs (see Plate 4–28) posed a difficult problem. Since there was no natural break in the design, a butt joint would be visible, but of course that solution was preferable to replacing the entire rear post.

The rear posts were sawed off just above the damaged area. In each case, a 1-inch hole was bored on center and into the leg stock, just as was done for the front leg and foot. Old cherry was used to make an extender with dowel approximately 1 inch in diameter and 4 inches long. The extender was attached to the rear post by inserting the dowel in the hole and applying glue to the joint (Plate 4–45). After the glue dried, a hand plane was used to taper the extender block to match the taper of the leg (Plate 4–46).

The broken drawer divider (see Plate 4–29) found on this piece is an example of another type of damage that commonly occurs. Although it would have been easier to replace the entire piece, the cost would have been greater, in that an original part of the work would have been lost. As a first step, an area the exact size of the tenon was cut back into the drawer divider (Plate 4–47). An extender was then fitted into the slot and glued (Plate 4–48). Finally, the extender was worked down to the proper size;

PLATE 4–44

The drawer shown on Plate 4–26b completely restored.

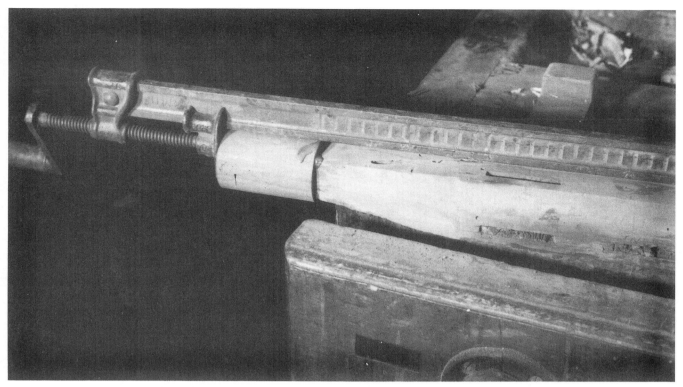

PLATE 4–45

The length extender being glued to the rear leg. It did not have to be round, but just happened to be an old piece of cherry that was available.

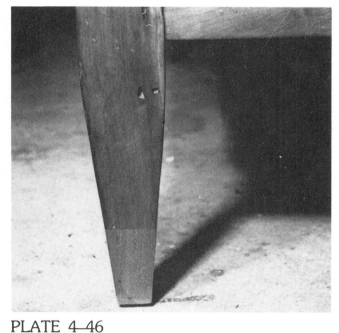

PLATE 4–46

The repaired rear leg. The very faint butt joint can be seen. The unseen dowel in the leg provides the needed strength.

PLATE 4–47

Removing a section of the drawer divider so that a new tenon can be attached.

PLATE 4-48

The new tenon fitted and in place.

PLATE 4-49

The new tenon cut to length and formed to fit the wear groove in the drawer divider.

even the contour of the wear caused by the opening and closing of the drawer was copied (Plate 4-49).

"Floating tenons" had to be used to repair the upper and lower rear rails. That is, since the tenons on the rail had been broken off (see Plate 4-30), they had to be rebuilt in much the same manner as the tenon for the drawer divider. Mortises were cut into the rails, but they were hidden. Tenons were then made to fit both the new mortises and the original mortises that had been cut into the post many years ago. Plate 4-50 shows the top of the rear post with the original mortises visible, the two floating tenons, and the newly cut mortises in the rear rail.

As mentioned earlier, the single-board top is a particularly striking feature of the chest.

PLATE 4–50

*Floating tenons prepared and ready to be assembled in the rails
and legs of the chest.*

PLATE 4–51

*The warp in the top must be brought out by letting
the top lie in the sun.*

Plates 4–51 and 4–52 show the damage that existed. The warp was removed by putting the top (bowed side up) out in the sun under a piece of glass. The seasoned crack (Plate 4–52) could have been removed by ripping the top and regluing it. However, to preserve the single board, a large plug was used to cover as much of the damage as possible. Since the top was originally nailed in place, square nails could be placed in the original holes to secure the top to the chest. The repair work to the damaged area is illustrated in Plates 4–53 to 4–57. Plate 4–58 shows the top, free of warp, fastened to the chest. (The restored chest can be seen in Plate 6–4).

PLATE 4–52

Other damage to the top includes seasoning cracks, splits caused by nails, and stress cracks caused by moisture.

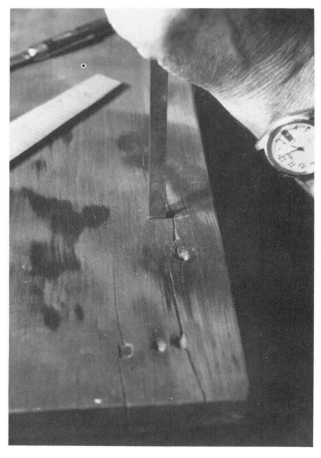

PLATE 4–53

Scribing the outline of the patch plug.

PLATE 4–54

A cut approximately ¼ inch deep is made along the scribe line with a chisel and mallet. The scribe lines that run across the grain should be cut first to reduce the chance of splitting the wood beyond the scribe lines.

PLATE 4–56

After the plug has been tested for fit, it can be glued in place. A thick piece of wood is placed between the jaws of the clamp and the plug to distribute pressure evenly over the entire surface of the plug.

PLATE 4–55

Once the cut has been made around the edges of the area to be covered, the surface of the area within the boundaries of the scribe marks is removed.

PLATE 4–57

The plug in place and dressed down so that it is even with the surface of the top.

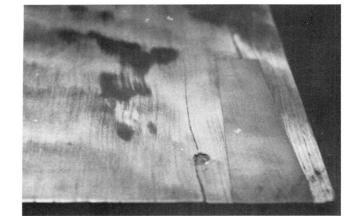

PLATE 4–58

The repaired top fastened to the finished chest.

Some Other Repairs

When drawers become stuck, breaks often occur in the pins on the through-dovetail joint that holds the sides to the back of the drawer (Plate 4–59). The steps used to ensure that the original stock is preserved are illustrated in Plates 4–60 to 4–64.

If drawer sides and supports are worn, but not to the extent that the drawers are split or will not open easily, repairs should not be made. The examples in Plates 4–65 and 4–66 illustrate such wear.

PLATE 4–59

Common damage when a stuck drawer is forced: broken pins from the dovetail joint that holds the back of the drawer to the sides.

PLATE 4–60

A notch is cut in the back board exactly where the pins were.

PLATE 4–61

Extenders fitted and glued in the notches.

Another type of wear that often turns up can be seen in the Windsor chairs in Plate 4–67. Among other damage, they all have one feature in common: the legs have worn down to the point where the chair seat is only 15 inches or less above the floor. All early Windsor chairs had seats that were from 17 to 17½ inches above the floor. In this case, the length of the legs was restored by means of an extender made with a dowel that was fitted in a hole bored in the end of the legs. Extreme care must be taken in making this type of repair since the diameter of the original stock is limited. The hole bored to receive a dowel should not have a diameter more than half the smallest diameter of the stock being bored. The procedure used in restoring the legs to their proper length is illustrated in Plates 4–68 to 4–75.

PLATE 4–62

Extenders dressed down to the correct thickness and length.

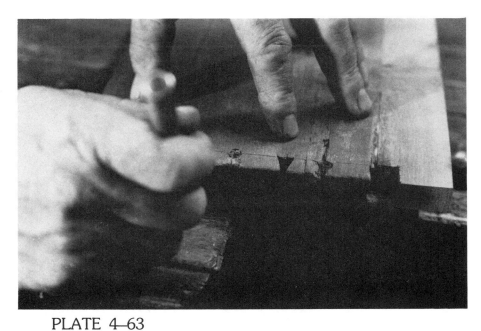

PLATE 4–63

Drawer back is aligned over the end of the drawer side to which it will be attached, and the location and shape of the pins is scribed; the drawer side is used as the guide.

PLATE 4–64

The drawer assembled. Notice the extenders and how they were shaped to fit onto the dovetails in the side piece.

PLATE 4–65

A drawer that shows considerable wear, but is still usable and therefore should not be repaired.

PLATE 4–66

A drawer guide and support showing wear but are still usable and therefore should not be repaired.

PLATE 4–67

A cluster of Windsor chairs waiting for restoration.
(Courtesy of Seabury Antiques.)

PLATE 4–69

Hole bored into the leg to receive the dowel on the
length extender.

PLATE 4–68

Truing the leg before the length extender is to be
attached.

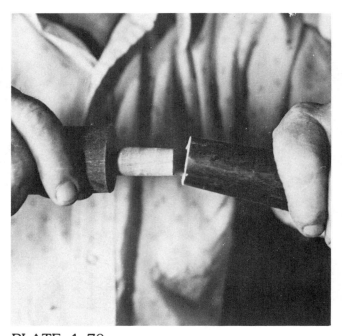

PLATE 4–70

Testing the dowel on the extender for proper fit.

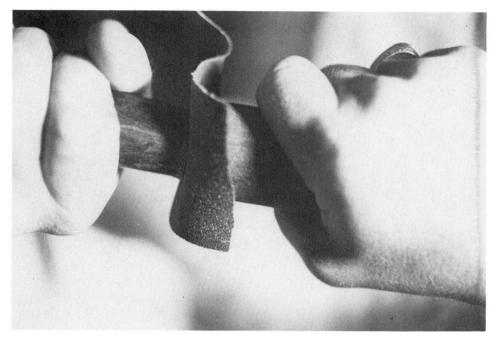

PLATE 4–71

Dressing down the face of the leg to assure the best fit between the end grain of the leg and the extender.

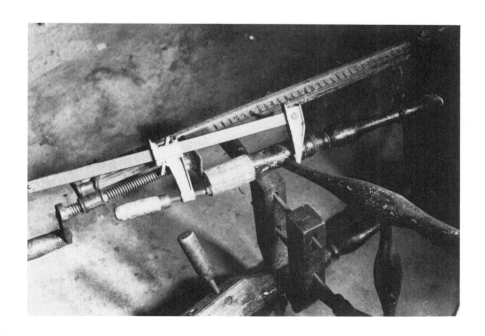

PLATE 4–72

Clamping the extenders in place.

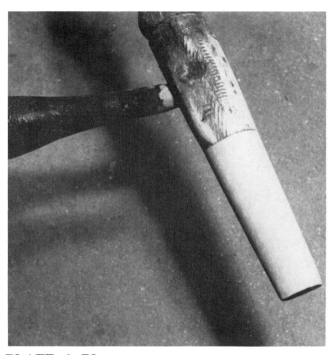

PLATE 4–73

Shaping the extender to match the profile of the leg.

PLATE 4–74

Coloring the extender to match the finish on the original work.

PLATE 4–75

The chair returned to its normal height of 17½ inches from the seat to the floor.

Notice in Plate 4–71 how the end grain of the extender block was fitted to the leg. A piece of sandpaper with a hole the size of the dowel cut in it was placed over the dowel, the grain side facing the original leg stock. By rotating the paper with the extender through a 10-degree arc it was possible to remove the irregular high points on the face of the leg and to ensure a close fit. Plate 4–72 shows the extenders clamped in place while the chairs are being assembled. A word of caution should be mentioned here, however: Windsor chairs should not be taken apart unless it is absolutely necessary to do so.

It is not feasible here to cover every type of damage that can come to a piece of furniture. If, however, the craftsperson can identify the category of the damage and can follow the procedures outlined in Chapter 1, the repair efforts should be successful—and satisfying.

I include the following because it illustrates a treatment of damage that is somewhat out of the ordinary. The piece is a chest of drawers that has a full-turned post down the front. The undamaged companion post shows that the post terminates with a half-round ball. It is that part

PLATE 4–76
Damaged Area.

of the turning that has rotted away (Plate 4–76). It would be tempting to remove the entire foot below the square and replace from that point down. However, upon close inspection the original break in the design where the tapered portion of the design ended and the half-round ball began can still be seen. Rather than lose that much original work, I choose to cut away the damaged part where the original shoulder existed, and start the repair work there (Plate 4–77). Second, I bored a hole up into the foot to receive the dowel that has been turned on the replacement piece, which is also shown in Plate 4–77. It is then a simple matter of gluing the replacement part to the original stock. By doing the repair as illustrated, very little of the original stock was lost. Always study the damaged section very closely before starting repairs. Plate 4–78 shows the repaired foot, complete with stain and finish.

PLATE 4–77
Damaged foot ready for repairs.

PLATE 4–78
Repaired foot.

5

Replacing What Has Been Lost

When approaching a piece of furniture that has some part missing, do so with a positive attitude. If the piece is of any value, and worth the time, it probably can be repaired. Remember that you are fighting what seems to be some kind of disease of antiquity that causes tables to lose at least one leg, a chest to lose a drawer, a crown mold to fall off, at least one hinge to be broken, most of the original hardware to be gone, and the top of a blanket chest to be either damaged or missing. In the discussion that follows, I have chosen to illustrate the replacement of those parts that are most often lost. Of course, some parts, such as the top to a table, require only cutting replacement stock to the correct size and securing to the piece being restored. Such replacement work does not require extensive discussion, only the good luck of finding a single board wide enough to make the top.

Replacing a Lost Turning

A turned leg table with a leg missing gives a first impression of being a lost cause. To replace a turning, the craftsperson only needs to get a good pattern from an original and duplicate it on a lathe. This is not as difficult as it may seem. The first thing you need to do is make what I call a profile board. To do this, cut a piece of ¼-inch plywood or other material to the exact length and width of the original piece. In the photographs I have used a piece of plywood

with a paper cover. I used the paper for the purpose of illustration, and it is not normally required. On the profile board, scribe a centerline from one end to the other. Placing the profile board parallel to the original turning, and using a square, transfer each distinct breakpoint of the design onto the profile board. Square a line across the profile board at these points. This is shown in Plate 5–1. If the design has a long flowing taper, make several check points along this section of the design. At these points you can use a parting tool to make reference cuts. Do not go to the final diameter at this time. Make these lines every 2 or 3 inches along the design. Using calipers, measure the diameter of the leg at all reference lines and note the measurement on the profile board (Plate 5–2). These noted mea-

PLATE 5–1

Setting the lines on a profile board.

PLATE 5–2

Noting diameter measurements.

PLATE 5–4

Finished profile board.

surements will be very helpful once the turning has begun. At each reference line, locate points half the diameter measurement to the left and right of the centerline. Plate 5–3 shows a craftsperson laying out such points.

Trusting your eye, connect these profile points with a line using the original turning as a model. Plate 5–4 shows the transferring of the design onto the profile board. By doing this you have a readily available reference from which to work.

Once you are satisfied with the profile board, select the stock that is to be used to turn the replacement part. Align the profile board with the turning stock and locate all transfer lines that identify where the original design moved from a full square stock to a turn. Place the stock in the lathe and using a skew chisel on its edge, score the corners of the stock on the lines that identify the termination of square stock (see Plate 5–5). Referring to Plate 5–5, the area of the stock to the left of the line is to remain square, while

PLATE 5–3

Laying out the profile points.

PLATE 5–5

Scoring the corners with a skew.

the area to the right of the line will be turned to a round. Scoring the corners as shown will prevent splintering the wood up into the square portion once the turning process begins.

Plate 5–6 illustrates the use of a parting tool to separate further that portion of the stock that is to remain square from that portion of the stock that is to be made round. From this point in the process it is a matter of reducing the remaining stock to a complete round.

Once the stock has been brought to round, place the profile board against the turning stock and locate the remaining reference points (Plate 5–7). Hold a pencil to each point, and rotate the stock by hand and scribe a line around the stock (Plate 5–8). This makes it possible to see the points while the stock is rotating.

From this point different people have different approaches to the turning. I prefer to lay the profile board above and behind the turning

PLATE 5–6
Cutting the shoulder of the square.

PLATE 5–7
Setting reference points.

PLATE 5–8

Setting reference lines.

so that I can keep it in my field of vision. I then take a parting tool and cut all shoulders to the correct diameter. When possible, I try to get a rough profile of the entire pattern on the stock, but oversize. Gradually, I bring each part down to the correct diameter, often measuring with the calipers as I do so. Plates 5–9 to 5–11 show the progress of the turning. Notice in Plate 5–10 how the tapered section of the design has been divided into four sections. It can also be seen where I have made three reference cuts with the parting tool to obtain the correct diameter. I continue to work the stock until it matches the original. The final step is to sand the work

PLATE 5–9

Turning shoulders and beads.

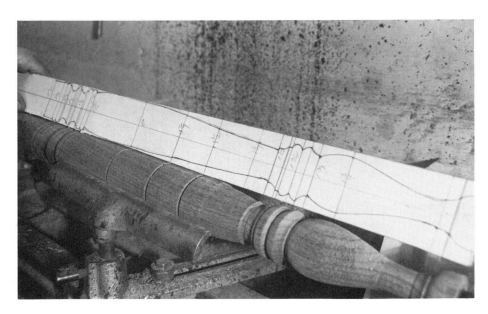

PLATE 5–10

Checking the progress with the profile board.

PLATE 5–11

Comparing the replacement part with an original part.

while it is turning in the lathe. Care should be taken not to remove the finer features of the turning with heavy sanding.

Making an Ogee Bracket Foot

An ogee bracket foot is a most graceful and beautiful bit of furniture architecture. It was introduced in the eighteenth century, with much credit for its development being given to John Goddard. Goddard, a celebrated cabinetmaker, was an active builder and designer of furniture from 1745 to 1785. His drawings are considered as standards in furniture design. When the ogee bracket foot is incorporated into the design of furniture that normally sat against the wall, the feet on the front corners of the piece will be full ogee type, allowing the design to wrap around the corner of the work. A single face or half ogee bracket foot will be at the rear corners, allowing the piece to set flat against the wall. Desks that sat out in the center of a room will have full ogee bracket feet at each corner, giving the piece a beautiful, rich appearance.

In making the ogee bracket foot, I will use a technique that will allow for a nearly perfect match of the feet, as well as providing a very strong foot. (See the insert for Plate 6–13). As you will see, I make use of a modern table saw with an auxilliary fence for the work. Extreme care must be taken while using the saw in this manner. If the craftsperson does not have an excellent command of the table saw, I cannot recommend that this method be used. An alter-native method would be the use of the molding planes shown earlier. The nomenclature of an ogee bracket foot is illustrated in Figure 5–1. The height (h dimension) of the bracket foot is usually 4 to 6 inches, with the wing running out as much as 8 to 10 inches, depending on the width of the piece to which it is attached. The toe of the foot should never protrude beyond the vertical plane of the convex portion at the top of the foot.

FIGURE 5–1

Nomenclature of an ogee bracket foot.

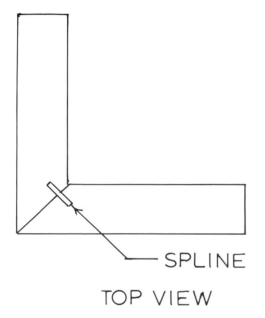

SPLINE

TOP VIEW

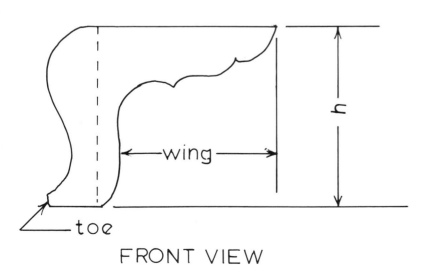

FRONT VIEW

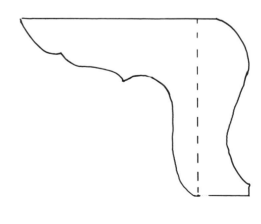

SIDE VIEW

If any remnants of the original feet exist, take as much information as possible concerning size and pattern. If there are no remnants, consider the following. If the chest on which you are planning to replace the ogee bracket feet is approximately 42 inches wide and 48 inches tall, the feet need to be at least 5 inches tall with an 8-inch wing. A massive piece of furniture such as a secretary with a bookcase above should have a foot with a height that will place the writing surface 30 inches above the floor and a 10-inch wing. A small 36-inch chest of drawers will have a foot that is 4½ inches tall and a 6-inch wing. These are examples. Let your eye help in determining the correct proportions. It might be wise to make a scale drawing. You can cut the profile of an ogee bracket foot from cardboard and test the proportions.

In the following a complete set of bracket feet will be constructed, including two double-face and two single-face feet. Let's go at this in steps.

Step 1. Once you have determined the size of the ogee bracket foot, select three pieces of stock. The wood should be wide enough to accommodate the desired height of the foot, and of length twice the distance from the tip of the wing to the toe plus an extra inch or two.

Step 2. Cut miters on both ends of one piece and on one end of the remaining two pieces (Plate 5–12).

Step 3. Cut splines near the inside face of the miters (Plate 5–13). The splines should

PLATE 5–12

Cutting miters for the foot stock.

PLATE 5–13

Cutting spline for the foot stock.

be within ½ to ¾ of an inch in from the inside surface of the stock. If the spline is placed out very far, the cutting of the concave portion of the ogee design might go deep enough to expose the splines.

Step 4. On the two pieces having only one miter joint, cut a rabbet joint on the inside surface and on the opposite end from the miter joints. Once again, the rabbet joint should not go more than ¾ of an inch in depth or else the concave portion of the ogee design might expose the rabbet joints. The cutting of the rabbet joints are shown in Plates 5–14 and 5–15. Notice that the saw guard has been removed to provide a clear view of the work.

Step 5. Cut a retainer board to support the back side of the assembly. This retainer board should be long enough to keep the assembly square. If we were making a bracket foot with all the feet being doubled face, the retainer board would be replaced with the heavy stock, and all pieces would have miters cut on both ends. Plate 5–16 shows all the pieces ready for trial assembly.

Step 6. Cut the splines and trial fit the assembly of the pieces. Measure and cut the spline stock so that the grain runs across the miter joint. This is illustrated in Figure 5–2. Plate 5–17 shows the pieces assembled. The scrap piece across the front is notched to provide

PLATE 5–14

Making the shoulder cut for a rabbet joint.

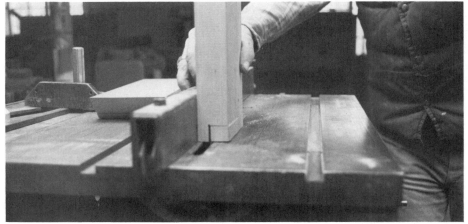

PLATE 5–15

Making the depth cut for a rabbet joint.

PLATE 5–16

Stock ready for trial assembly.

PLATE 5–17

Trial fitting of the assembly.

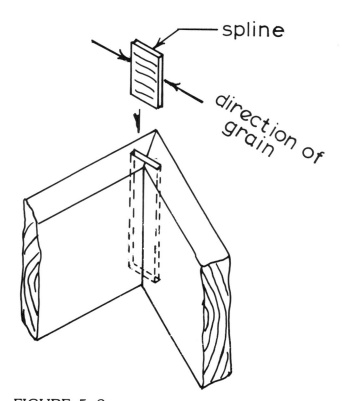

FIGURE 5–2

Preparing the spline for a spline joint.

a very tight fit and prevent spreading of the assembled work when pressure is applied. This block replaces a clamp and makes the gluing process much easier.

Step 7. Glue the assembly, being sure that it remains square.

Step 8. After the glue has set, remove the stock from the clamps, and draw the profile of the ogee pattern on the sides of the assembly. This will provide a reference once the cutting of the concave portion of the ogee is started.

Let's pause to discuss the auxiliary fence setup. Plate 5–18 shows the auxiliary fence positioned on the table saw. The fence is a sturdy straightedge. Notice that as the stock is moved along the fence it will approach the blade from a side angle. The blade should be a heavy-duty coarse rip blade. I have found that a chisel-shaped carbon-tipped blade does well.

Step 9. Set the blade to where it barely protrudes above the top of the table saw.

PLATE 5–18

Set up for an auxiliary fence.

Step 10. Turn the saw on and make a pass across the blade, scoring all three sides. If you have the saw set too deep or are pushing the stock into the blade too fast, the blade will tend to ring. Listen for this sound and adjust your work accordingly.

Step 11. Raise the saw blade about ¹⁄₁₆ of an inch and pass the stock over the blade a second time, again scoring all three sides. Continue to make passes, observing the progress toward the outline of the pattern. It may be necessary to change the angle of the auxiliary fence as you proceed. As more of the blade becomes exposed above the table, you will find that it will be necessary to decrease the amount by which the height of the blade is increased for each run. The process shown in Plates 5–19, 5–20, 5–21 shows the progress of cutting the concave portion of the ogee design.

Step 12. Use a block plane to work out the convex portion of the design (Plate 5–22).

PLATE 5–19

Completion of the initial run.

PLATE 5–20

The concave surface—partially completed.

PLATE 5–21

The final run in forming the concave surface.

PLATE 5–22

Step 13. Draw the profile of the foot on the inside face of the stock as shown in Plate 5–23. Notice how the pattern has been folded. As the pattern was made for the outside surface of the foot and the wing is being laid out on the inside surface, it is necessary to fold the pattern as shown.

Step 14. Separate the individual feet by cutting the sides as shown in Plate 5–24.

Step 15. The design of the profile may be cut using a coping saw or a power scroll saw. The retainer board used earlier can now be cut to some form of brace and attached to the rear feet. The brace can be secured to the back edge of the cabinet and will provide much needed support for the piece of furniture. The completed set of ogee bracket feet are illustrated in Plate 5–25.

PLATE 5–23

Drawing the profile of the foot.

PLATE 5–24

Separating the individual feet.

PLATE 5–25
Set of ogee bracket feet.

Constructing a Drawer Using a Dovetail Joint

We want to remember that when replacing a part of a piece of furniture, not only are we to make the piece useful, but we want to do the replacement work so that it will not be noticeable. How to construct a half-lap multiple dovetail joint will be illustrated using a flush front drawer and a lipped front drawer. The half-lap multiple dovetail joint is the most desirable and most difficult type of drawer construction. Other types of drawer construction are discussed in my book, *Making Country Furniture* (Prentice Hall, Inc., 1986, Englewood Cliffs, N.J.).

The most obvious thing is to use the same kind of wood as is in the original piece. Just as important is to match the style of work of the maker. Before starting to replace a drawer, observe the type of joints used on the original drawers, and copy exactly. In the case of a dovetail drawer, study the layout used by the original builder, and duplicate. Some people used a very wide dovetail and extremely narrow pins. Even though this does not give the strongest joint, if the original work used such a style, it should be copied. Examples of styles of dovetail joints are shown in Plate 5–26.

Select the stock for the front, and reduce it to the proper thickness. The thickness is normally ⅞ of an inch. Again, if an original drawer is available, match the thickness of the front used on the original. Reduce the width and length of the replacement front so that it will fit into the intended opening with a clearance approximately the thickness of a dime all the way around. It is extremely important to do this, in that the size of the drawers is taken from the drawer front. If the front does not fit, the drawer will not fit. From this point let's consider the procedure in steps of operation.

PLATE 5–26
Styles of joints.

Step 1. Select the sides for the drawers, and reduce to the proper thickness.

Step 2. Cut the sides to the same width as the drawer front.

Step 3. Square one end of each of the side stock. Do not be concerned about the exact length at this time.

Step 4. Scribe a line on the inside face of the drawer front that is in from the end a distance equal to the thickness of the drawer sides plus about 1/32 of an inch (see Plate 5–27).

Step 5. Scribe a line across the inside and outside face of the drawer sides in from the end a distance that is equal to about seven-eighths of the thickness of drawer front (see Plate 5–28).

Step 6. Using the same setting on the marking gauge and with the head of the gauge against the inside face of the drawer front, scribe a line on the end grain of the drawer front. Do this on both ends. This is shown in Plate 5–29.

Step 7. Lay out the profile of the dovetails on the side stock.

PLATE 5–28

Setting the length of the dovetails onto the side stock.

PLATE 5–29

Setting the length of the dovetails on the front stock.

PLATE 5–27

Setting the depth for the mortises on the drawer front.

Let's talk about step 7 for a moment. If you have an original drawer to copy, use a sliding T-bevel to determine the slope of the dovetails, as shown in Plate 5–30. If you do not have an original drawer to copy, I suggest the following procedure.

PLATE 5–30

Determining the slope of the dovetails from an existing drawer.

1. Determine the number of dovetails to be cut and divide the end into that many equal sections.
2. Square lines at these division points across the end of the side stock as shown in Figure 5–3.
3. To determine the slope of the dovetail, mark off six spaces as shown in Figure 5–4a, and at the sixth division point lay a perpendicular line to the edge of the board that is one division long. Draw a line from the edge of the board where the line started through point A. Adjust the sliding T-bevel to this angle (Figure 5–4b). This will give a 6:1 slope.
4. Lay out the dovetails as shown in Figure 5–4c, marking very plainly that part of the stock that is to be removed. In this illustration the darkened area is to be removed.

Regardless of the procedure used to locate the dovetails, mark all areas on all pieces that are to be removed. I use the letter "R" to indicate waste or removal stock. It is very easy to forget and remove the incorrect part of the layout. Also, when removing waste stock, do all cutting on the waste side of the lines.

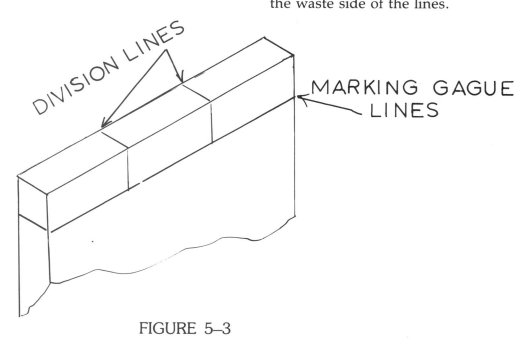

FIGURE 5–3

Determining the spacing of the dovetails.

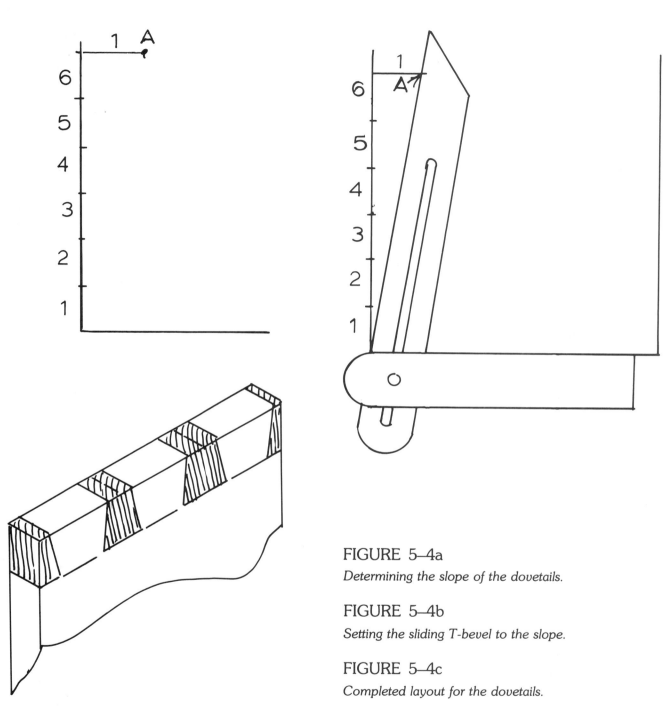

FIGURE 5–4a

Determining the slope of the dovetails.

FIGURE 5–4b

Setting the sliding T-bevel to the slope.

FIGURE 5–4c

Completed layout for the dovetails.

Plates 5–31 through 5–39 provide step-by-step guidelines for cutting a dovetail joint in a drawer. When transferring the dovetail outline to the front stock as shown in Plate 5–34, use a sharp knife or scriber. A pencil line will give too coarse a line, resulting in a poor fit. Alternate between the steps shown in Plate 5–36 and 5–37 until most of the waste stock has been removed. When finishing out the waste stock as shown in Plate 5–38, an ever-so-slight undercutting will give a very good joint. It is at this point in the process that you should begin to do some

PLATE 5–31

Making the shoulder cuts in the side stock.

PLATE 5–32

Cleaning out the waste with a coping saw.

PLATE 5–33

Truing up the cuts with a chisel.

PLATE 5–34

Preparing to transfer the dovetail outline to the front stock.

PLATE 5–35

Making the shoulder cuts on the mortises to receive the dovetails.

PLATE 5–36

Starting the removal of waste by making a chisel cut at the depth line about ¼ of an inch deep. Since wood splits with the grain, making this cut first will minimize the possibility of splitting beyond the desired point.

PLATE 5–37

Removing some of the waste stock by gently tapping a chisel with a mallet.

PLATE 5–38

True up the sides and bottom of the mortise using a sharp chisel and hand pressure.

PLATE 5–39

Trial fitted dovetail joint.

trial fitting of the side stock to the front stock. Plate 5–39 shows a trial assembly of the dovetail joint.

Cutting the Groove for the Drawer Bottom

Once the joint between the drawer front and the drawer sides has been constructed, the groove for the bottom needs to be cut. The groove must be located in the center of the bottom dovetail. By doing this the groove will be hidden completely.

Step 1. Set the blade on a table saw to a depth that is about half the thickness of the side stock.

Step 2. Adjust the saw fence so that with the bottom edge of the drawer front against the fence, the saw blade will cut a groove in the center of the bottom dovetail mortise (see Plate 5–40).

Step 3. Working with the bottom edge of the drawer front and drawer sides against the fence, cut a groove down the length of the pieces. If a wider groove is needed, adjust the fence out slightly and make multiple runs. A dado head could be used here. A word of caution.

PLATE 5–40

Cutting the groove for the bottom.

Clearly mark on each piece where the groove is to be cut. I know from experience that it is very easy to forget and cut the groove on the incorrect face or side of the stock.

Plate 5–41 shows the progress of the work on the drawer to this point.

PLATE 5–41

Halflap dovetail joints and groove for the drawer bottom.

PLATE 5–42

Determining the length of the sides.

Placing the Back on the Drawer

The stock for the back of the drawer should have the same thickness as the stock for the sides of the drawer. The length of the back stock should be the same as the length for the drawer front. The width of the drawer back should be the same as the distance from the top of the groove for the bottom, to the top of the drawer side. The dovetails that are used on the back of the drawer are called through dovetails in that the dovetails and pins extend through the full thickness of the stock. Joining the drawer sides to the drawer back is done as follows.

Step 1. Determine the correct length for the drawer sides. To do so, assemble one drawer side to the front. Measuring from the outside of the drawer front, mark a point on the drawer side a distance that is equal to the depth of the piece of furniture in which the drawer will be placed. Square and cut the side stock to this length. This is shown in Plate 5–42. In this case the depth is 18 inches.

Step 2. Using a marking gauge set to the thickness of the side and back stock, and with the head of the gauge against the end of the stock for the back, scribe a line on both faces of both ends of the stock, as shown in Plate 5–43.

PLATE 5–43

Setting the depth for the pins on a drawer back.

Step 3. With the head of the marking gauge against the back end of the side pieces, scribe a similar line on both faces of the side stock (see Plate 5–44).

Step 4. In the same manner in which dovetails were laid out on the front end of the drawer sides, lay out two or three dovetails on the back ends of side stock (Plate 5–45). Notice that the dovetails are so located that when the bottom pin is cut on the back stock, it will be a half-pin.

Step 5. Remove the waste area using the technique described earlier, leaving the dovetails.

PLATE 5–44

Setting the length of dovetails on drawer side stock.

PLATE 5–46

Locating the rear pins for the drawer back.

PLATE 5–45

Locating the dovetails on the drawer sides.

PLATE 5–47

Laying out the pins for back stock of the drawer.

Step 6. Align the side stock with the back stock and transfer the pattern of the dovetails onto the end grain of the back stock (Plate 5–46).

Step 7. Square lines down the face of the back stock to meet the scribe line made earlier (Plate 5–47).

Step 8. Using the back saw and the coping saw, remove the waste stock, being sure to work on the waste side of the pattern lines.

Step 9. Plate 5–48 shows the assembled joint for the drawer back and side.

PLATE 5–48

Drawer back and side assembly.

Plate 5–49 shows the assembled drawer with a cutaway of the bottom to illustrate how the bottom fits into the groove. The bottom should be about ½ inch thick, with the edges tapered to fit into the grooves. The bottom must be wide enough to extend under the drawer back. It can thus be secured with nails through the bottom and into the edge grain of the back.

Constructing a Lipped-Front Drawer

The drawer construction discussed earlier was the type in which the drawer fit flush with the front of the cabinet. A lipped front drawer has a small lip around the drawer, causing the drawer to protrude from the front of the cabinet slightly. This type of drawer may have evolved from a box type of drawer being constructed using rather crude joints. To hide the joints and provide an attractive front, an oversized piece of stock was fastened to the box drawer. This formed the lip. The only difference in the construction of the lipped front drawer and the flush front drawer is in the design of the drawer front. I will discuss this difference only. For construction techniques beyond the points covered here, refer to the discussion on the flush front drawer.

Plates 5–50 and 5–51 illustrate how the lip front is formed from a single piece of stock using a table saw. The stock for the lip front needs to be at least 1⅛ inches thick. The saw guard has been removed to show the view. In Plate 5–50 a cheek cut is being made around the drawer front. This cut is down both sides and across both ends. Plate 5–51 shows the shoulder cut. From these two cuts the lip is formed.

The rabbet plane is then used to remove the saw marks and finish fit the drawer to the opening for which it is being made (see Plate 5–52). As it was necessary to be sure that the drawer front on a flush drawer fit the opening properly, it is also necessary for the raised portion of the lipped drawer to fit the opening properly. It is from the raised part of the front that measurements for the sides and back are taken.

Once the drawer front fits the opening, the stock for the drawer sides can be secured and cut to the correct width. This can be done in the same manner that drawer sides were made for the flush drawer. When laying out the dovetails for the lipped drawer, the length of the dovetails will be the same as the shoulder depth of the lipped drawer. Once the dovetails have

PLATE 5–50

Making the cheek cut for a lipped drawer front.

PLATE 5–51

Making the shoulder cut for a lipped drawer front.

PLATE 5–52

Dressing the drawer front for proper fit.

PLATE 5–53

Laying out dovetail mortises on drawer front.

been cut, their outline can be traced onto the end grain of the drawer front as shown in Plate 5–53.

Using the same method that was used on the flush drawer, cut the mortises for the dovetails. Notice in Plate 5–54 that the lip shows a

slight nick caused by the back saw when the shoulders of the mortises were being cut. This is a common feature for hand-cut joints. Plate 5–55 shows the dovetails fitted into the mortises.

The remaining construction needed for the drawer is done in the same manner as was used

PLATE 5–54

Dovetail mortises cut on a lipped drawer front.

PLATE 5–55

Assembled dovetail joint.

on the flush front drawer. The groove for the drawer bottom should be centered on the bottom dovetail. The drawer back should be secured in the same manner as was done for the flush-front drawer.

Locating and Cutting a Mortise Joint

Earlier in this chapter a leg was turned to replace one that had been lost. For the new leg to be of use, mortise joints must be made to receive the tenon of the table rail. Plates 5–56 and 5–57 illustrate how the mortise in one of the original legs is being used as a guide for laying out the mortise in the new leg. Although one of the original legs may be used to duplicate the mortise as far as size and distance from the end of the leg are concerned, the craftsperson must be careful to lay out the mortise from the correct edge and on the correct surface. Otherwise, you may end up with two left rear legs or two right front legs or some other duplicating combination.

PLATE 5–57

Determining the width and offset of a mortise using original work as a guide.

For the operation shown in Plate 5–56, the replacement leg is secured in line with one of the original legs, and the points identifying the length of the mortise are transferred to the new stock using a square and scriber. Then set a marking gauge according to the scribed lines on the original leg and mark the location and width of the mortise on the new leg. The original gauge marks can be seen on the old stock in the illustration in Plate 5–57. The completed transfer of markings are shown in Plate 5–58. I have placed a large × on the new stock to indicate the area that is to be removed.

Plate 5–59 reveals that I have bored out most of the waste stock for the mortise. Although there is evidence that early cabinetmakers chiseled this stock out, there is also evidence that many of the early makers did bore out most of the waste stock. A chisel was then used to square the sides of the mortise. By using the drill to remove much of the waste stock, I have not broken from the traditional methods. Using a chisel, the sides of the mortise can be trued. The results of this work are illustrated in Plate 5–60. Using a chisel that is slightly less wide than the mortise, I cut along the top and bottom scribe lines. By making

PLATE 5–56

Locating the mortise length using original work as a guide.

PLATE 5–58

The location of the mortises on the replacement stock.

PLATE 5–59

Removing waste stock by boring.

PLATE 5–60

The completed mortise.

these cuts first, the chance of splitting out the wood is minimized. Using a mallet, I drive the chisel about half the depth of the mortise. Second, I use a wider chisel and cut along the side scribe lines. Most often this cut can be done with hand pressure. Again I take this cut down about half the depth of the mortise. How deep you cut depends on the hardness of the stock. I then return to the top and bottom of the mortises and take those cuts to the bottom of the mortise. I finish out the work by bringing the side cuts to the bottom of the mortise. As you go through the foregoing operations, it may be necessary periodically to remove the stock from the bench vise and shake out the shavings. With minor trimming the forming of the mortise should be completed.

Replacing the Swing Rail on a Gateleg Table

I have found that any part of a piece of furniture that has movement, such as drawers, doors, and drop leaves on tables, naturally become worn, broken, and sometimes lost. A moveable part that is no exception to this phenomenon is the swing rail of a gateleg table. It is quite a simple matter to swing the gateleg hurriedly out from under the table and catch the leg on a rug or the floor. This will place considerable stress on the mortise-and-tenon joint that secures the leg to the rail, and it will also place the hinge pins in a considerable bind. Eventually, the pin or the mortise-and-tenon joint will break. This would prompt the owner to remove the drop leaf and the gateleg and rail. In fact, it was not uncommon for both leaves to be removed at this time, providing the owner with a smaller usable table.

Plate 5–61 shows the side rail of a gateleg table. As can be seen, half of the hinge is still on the main rail. Although not very obvious, deep gouges have been cut in the main rail between the knuckles. This was done to provide clearance when the gate rail was swung out.

PLATE 5–61

Anchor rail for a swing rail.

First the replacement stock is to be secured. Then it is necesary to mark the locations of the knuckles on the replacement stock. This is shown in Plate 5–62. The correct length for the knuckles are determined next. The two pieces of stock should now be butted together, and the stock that is to be removed should be identified. This is

PLATE 5–62

Locating the knuckles for the swing rail.

shown in Plate 5–63. Notice that I have indicated with an R the stock that is to be removed. Failure to do this will increase a hundredfold the chance that the craftsperson will remove the wrong sections. Cut the knuckles a bit oversized and file the wood for the final fit. A tight fit is desired (see Plate 5–64).

To ensure clearance when the gate rail is swung out, the undersides of the sockets on the swing rail are cut out. Plate 5–65 shows the shoulder of the knuckle being cut back, and Plate 5–66 illustrates the use of a chisel and mallet in the removal of stock. Notice that the cut is a long wedge shape, ending at the edge of the socket.

PLATE 5–63
The complete layout of the gateleg hinge.

PLATE 5–64
Filing for final fit.

PLATE 5–65
Preparing to undercut the sockets of a swing rail hinge.

PLATE 5–66

Removing the undercut for clearance of a swing rail hinge.

PLATE 5–67

Drill the pin hole for a gateleg swing rail.

PLATE 5–68

Replaced swing rail for a gateleg table.

Once the replacement rail has been fitted properly to the original stock, the two pieces should be held in place and a pin hole drilled through the knuckles. Plate 5–67 shows a modern drill press being used for this task. The completed task is shown in Plate 5–68.

Forming a Molding

The molding that is being made in this section is for a small cupboard. Since early moldings were done by hand, and usually only enough

stock was worked up for each piece being constructed, molding variations found are limitless. If you observe the moldings closely, however, you will find that most early moldings incorporate a concave portion, a convex portion, shoulders, and beads. The pattern for the molding to be formed is shown in Plate 5–69. As can be seen, it starts with a bead at the top that goes into a shoulder. The shoulder goes into a concave section which then goes into another shoulder. The design is terminated with a half-convex section. The craftsperson may wish to work the molding down using molding planes for the entire process. I have found that it saves time and does not sacrifice quality if some of the bulk stock is removed by modern means. Plate 5–70

shows that a portion of the waste stock has been removed by setting the blade of a table saw to cut to the shoulders. I then use a modern rabbet plane to round out the bead. The rabbet plane is a unique tool in that the blade is of the same width as the bed of the plane. This allows the craftsperson to plane in corners. Use of the rabbet plane to help form the molding is shown in Plates 5–71 and 5–72. I then use my old round-nose molding plane to work out the concave portion of the design. This is shown in Plate 5–73. The finished work is shown in Plate 5–74.

I should mention that moldings can also be formed using a modern table saw and auxiliary fence. This technique was shown when discussing the making of an ogee bracket foot.

PLATE 5–69

Drawing the molding profile on the endgrain of the stock.

PLATE 5–70

Removing stock with a table saw.

PLATE 5–71

Using the rabbet plane to form the convex part of a bead.

PLATE 5–72

Using the rabbet plane to true the shoulders.

PLATE 5–73

Forming the concave portion of the design.

PLATE 5–74

Finished molding stock.

6

Examples of Restored Work

The great accomplishment of restoring an old piece of furniture is satisfying enough in itself, but the restorer has the added pleasure of being able to enjoy the fruits of his labor for years to come. In this chapter I present some examples of this effort (Plates 6–1 to 6–21). By and large the items chosen represent types of furniture that are still available to the average collector.

Certainly, much finer examples could have been found in museums or well-known collections, but the works shown here were chosen because they have never been featured in a book before and represent the kinds of furniture that can still be readily obtained. All of these items were found at auctions, flea markets, or antique shows, or through individual sellers in Indi-

PLATE 6–1

AMERICAN EMPIRE SECRETARY, CIRCA 1825

All of the features expected in a work of this type were found to be present: the framing joints are dovetail or mortise-and-tenon; the drawers consist of dovetail construction; the bottoms of the drawers are set in grooves in the sides and front of the drawer. Also, the veneer is very thick, the ends of the desk are single boards, and the brass has a deep luster with minute dents and scratches. The few pieces of original glass still present were very thin and filled with imperfections. (The loss of the glass certainly hurts the value of the piece.) The base of the desk is made of dark mahogany and is covered with mahogany veneer on the front edges. The bookcase portion, which is made of cherry, is also trimmed with mahogany veneer. The original cover is still on the writing surface. The mahogany feet are superbly carved. The work had never been painted and still carries its original finish.

ana, Illinois, Missouri, Ohio, or Kentucky. With the exception of the Shaker table shown in Plate 6–9, all of the pieces are from the writer's collection.

Each item, at the time of purchase, had some degree of damage. All repairs were done according to the rules and concepts presented in Chapter 3.

The dates given for each item, with the exception of the authenticated works, are not to be considered exact, but rather, are an approximation based on the features of the work.

PLATE 6–2

CHIPPENDALE STYLE SECRETARY, CIRCA 1790–1810

This work was so badly damaged and the repairs so extensive, that its antique value is lost. For reasons impossible to understand, someone had removed the drawers, cut out the drawer dividers, used the drawer fronts to make a bottom for the cavity, and hung two cheap pine doors. Restoration required putting in new drawer dividers, rebuilding the drawers, and putting new veneer on the fronts. All of the grill work was missing from the bookcase doors. Initial examination revealed that the veneer was extremely thick and that the core wood was San Domingo mahogany in the desk portion and cherry in the bookcase. All of the construction consisted of dovetails and mortise-and-tenon joints. All joints had been layed out by hand and the scribe marks were still visible. The brass hinges were cast, and the screws had off-center slots in the heads, fine threads, and a blunt end. Every aspect of the construction indicated that the piece was very old and very well made. It was therefore decided that restoration was justified even though the piece would no longer be considered a true antique.

PLATE 6–3

CHERRY CHEST OF DRAWERS, CIRCA 1800–1820

The chest is made of cherry, and the two large drawers at the top and the side post are trimmed with tiger maple. Not only does this work have all the classic marks of age, such as the wide dovetail drawer construction, but it has wood pegs in place of nails for screws to hold the work together. The locks are hammered iron, somewhat crudely made, which strongly suggest that this work was done during the British embargo of the United States during the early 1800s. The document drawer between the two bonnet drawers has a hidden compartment.

PLATE 6–4

CHEST OF DRAWERS, CIRCA 1830–1850

This is the chest featured in Chapter 4. As the photograph shows, the chest is once again serving its intended purpose.

PLATE 6–5
TEN-LEG BANQUET, CIRCA 1830

According to the seller, this table had been the object of a family feud. Two heirs had fought over it, and to settle the argument each person agreed to take one half with the understanding that neither would sell his half outside the family. In 1972 the table halves came back together with the settlement of the estate of the heirs. Inspection of the table revealed that the legs were not exactly alike and therefore had probably been turned by hand. In addition, the veneer around the band under the top was very thick, and thus old. The tops and drop leaves were single cherry boards, each more than 17 inches wide. The only problem with the table was that the two swing legs were missing. Nevertheless, the table was purchased. The twenty hours required to reproduce the two legs seemed a small price to pay to have the table whole again.

PLATE 6–6

EARLY SLAT-BACK CHAIR, AGE UNKNOWN

This chair was found in a woodpile in the barnyard of a farm outside of Louisville, Kentucky. It was made of a muted tiger maple, and was originally painted red. When it was purchased, practically all of the paint was gone. Unfortunately the original seat was lost, but other than that the chair was in perfect condition. It is easy to overlook a chair of this type. It is not as impressive as a Windsor or a bannister back, but it is just as desirable. It is very well proportioned, with a wide generous seat that is about 17 inches above the floor.

PLATE 6–7

DOVETAILED DOUGH BOX, CIRCA 1850

This box came from Madison, Indiana, and much of its history is known. In the quest for furniture, items of this type should not be overlooked. The fine dovetail type construction, and the delicate hand holes attest to the work of an early craftsman.

PLATE 6–8
WALNUT STEP CUPBOARD, CIRCA 1840

This cupboard was found in a yard sale in Springfield, Missouri. The seller said that it had come out of a log cabin and had been in the family for three generations. It is an excellent example of country workmanship. Even though it is fastened with squareheaded nails and appears to have been made with only a hammer, saw, and a square, it should not be considered primitive. The proportions of the major mass over the minor mass in the division of the front are superb. The inside bevel of the door panels, the pegged mortise-and-tenon joints, and the overall style indicate that the builder was a true craftsman. The use of nails is an acceptable method of holding the work together in a piece of this type, and no effort should be made to conceal them. The inset shows a simple, but graceful arch cut in the ends to form feet, and a well-made turnbuckle to fasten the doors. The only hardware consists of brass hinges (see Plate 2–23). This piece had never been painted, and required only minor repair on one door.

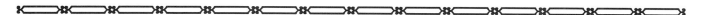

PLATE 6–9

SHAKER TILT-TABLE, CIRCA 1810

This table came from the West Union Shaker Community in Indiana, and was indeed on a trash truck headed for a landfill when it was spotted by a knowing person, and rescued. Of the works shown in this chapter, this table is one that is not easily obtained. Shaker furniture, especially items other than chairs, is very rare. Although the Shaker communities did sell many of their chairs to the outside world, other furniture items were made only for their own use. Therefore when Shaker items such as the table do appear, they have probably come from a sale that was held when one of the early communities was disbanded. Shaker items are simple and entirely functional. Needing to conserve time and space, Shakers designed the table so that it could be put out of the way when it was not being used. (Courtesy of Shaker Table Antiques.)

(a)

PLATE 6–10
SIX-BOARD PENNSYLVANIA DUTCH BLANKET CHEST, CIRCA 1820

This history of the chest is known, and the piece has been authenticated as a Pennsylvania Dutch blanket chest. Chests of this type will be made with wide boards, and the only joints are the dovetail joints at the corners. The hardware should be strap hinges, and the corners of the chest should be dovetailed together. Good examples will be either grain-painted or more elaborately designed with a scene of vivid colors. Unfortunately, in 1910, the owner of the chest attempted to remove the original paint. Not being successful, he decided to paint it white. When the white enamel was removed, only a faint pattern remained. Destroying the original finish reduced the value of the chest a hundredfold. This chest is a prime example of what not to do when refinishing. The inset shows the excellent through-dovetail construction of the bracket foot, and a faint indication that the feet were originally deep blue.

(b)

PLATE 6–11
BOW FRONT CHEST

The bow front chest shown in Plate 6–11 came to my attention through a friend. He warned me that it had been in a fire, and he was not sure that it could be restored. Having wanted a bow front for years, I could not pass up the opportunity to at least make the trip to see it. Upon inspection of the chest, I became convinced that it was indeed a very early work. It was obvious that most of the top had been destroyed. However, the finish appeared to be original, and although the chest was scorched over a greater part of its surface, I felt sure that most of the damage did not go below the many layers of shellac. Gambling that this was the case, I purchased the bow front chest. I used paint and varnish remover to strip most of the burned finish. I then used alcohol saturated steel wool to finish cleaning the surface. As I had hoped, most of the damage was to the finish only. I was able to save the bowed portion of the top, and only the back 12 inches of the top is a replacement board. It was necessary to replace some of the ribbon inlay around the edge of two of the drawers, and replace a small section of the apron. A burn stain can be seen on the right end of the top drawer, and a slight discoloration is noticeable on the right splay foot. The back being made of pine was badly charred, and should be replaced. However I choose to leave it for the time being. I refinished with many coats of oil. Sometimes taking a chance does pay.

(a)

PLATE 6–12
WALNUT TIP-TOP TEA TABLE, CIRCA 1790

When examining a table of this type, measure the top across grain and with the grain. If the work is old, the top should be narrow across grain owing to the shrinkage of the wood over the years. Also expect to find the legs secured to the pedestal with a dovetail joint, and reinforced with a hammered iron support (see insert). It is not uncommon to find a hardwood such as walnut used for the legs and pedestal, as is the case here, and pine or poplar used for the top. The only damage this table has sustained was caused by worms. The tip of one of the legs had deteriorated as well as the pivot block on which the top tilted. The leg that had not lost its full length was not repaired. However, it was necessary to replace the pivot block before the table could be functional (see inset). When worms are present in a piece of wood, effort should be made either to seal the wood or to treat it in some manner to kill the worms.

(c)

(b)

PLATE 6–13
CHEST OF DRAWERS, CIRCA 1750–1780

Never expect to see nails used as the principal means of construction in a work of this caliber. This work was constructed by attaching the ends to the top and bottom with open dovetail joints. The top, bottom, and both ends were made from single boards 18 inches wide. Except for the ogee bracket feet that were nearly worn away, the chest required only minor work on the drawers. To return the piece to its correct height and proportion, the worn feet were replaced by new ones fashioned from very old walnut. Enough of the original feet existed to determine the overall size and a part of the ogee pattern. The insert shows the ogee bracket foot reproduced in the same manner as the technique explained in Chapter 5.

(a)

(b)

(a)

PLATE 6–14
POST-AND-PANEL BLANKET CHEST, CIRCA 1850

Chests of this type usually had a top with a heavy cast iron hinge rather than a hammered strap hinge. Such pieces should have mortise-and-tenon joints, and the panels should be made of single boards. In this case, the panel is made of quarter-sawed cherry. The left rear foot of the chest has been eaten by worms, but its full length was not affected (see inset). Therefore no effort was made to replace the ball on the foot. If such damage does not affect the function or beauty of the work, the piece should be left as is. What better evidence of age?

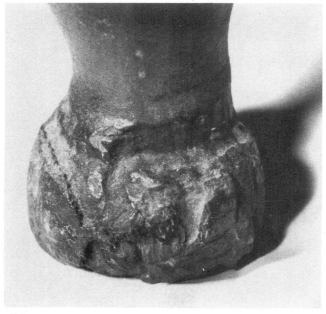

(b)

PLATE 6–16

WALNUT CORNER CABINET, CIRCA 1840

This work came from Madison, Indiana, and was authenticated as having been built around 1840. Pieces of this type are country furniture. It is acceptable for the face work to be secured with square nails. Expect to see evidence of hand plane marks on the door panels, and on the surface of the shelves. Plate grooves or small strips of wood nailed about 1 inch out from the back edge of the shelves are common features of this type of work. The hinges may be cast brass or iron, with wood turnbuckles to secure the doors. This piece is painted green on the inside.

PLATE 6–15

POPLAR STEP-BACK CUPBOARD, CIRCA 1840–1860

This work was probably painted or heavily stained at one time. The nails heads are recessed and covered with a filler. The hardware consists of mortised brass latches and cast iron hinges. The doors are constructed with through mortise-and-tenon joints. The full weight of the piece rests on the end boards, and the bracket foot is actually a facade.

PLATE 6–17
COUNTRY CUPBOARD, CIRCA 1850

This cupboard has an unusual arrangement of drawers, and was probably built to meet the needs of a particular person. Judging from the nails and hinges used, the above date was estimated. Had this work been done around 1900, Victorian hardware would probably have been used. Do not expect to see any tool marks other than those from a saw, hand plane, and chisel on work of this type and age. This work was found in central Indiana near the Illinois border. The only repairs needed were for typical wear on the drawers.

PLATE 6–18
DISH CUPBOARD, CIRCA 1890

The cabinet of this type of cupboard will commonly be secured with square nails and butt joints. The doors will be constructed with mortise-and-tenon joints. These joints may be pinned. The panels will be made from a single board and may be beveled on either the inside or outside surface. Occasionally the panels will be beveled on both sides. The work shown is painted red and has five shelves with plate grooves. Included in the picture is a cistern pump. The pump is painted green with yellow dolphins in the design.

PLATE 6–19

PRIMITIVE CHEST, CIRCA 1840

This chest was built by the writer's great grandfather. He was a night rider in Hopkins County, Kentucky, and he used this chest to store his cape, mask, and pistol. It was constructed using a saw, hammer, and nails. The right end of the top protrudes past the end of the box, and serves as a handle to lift the lid. On primitive work, expect to see out-of-square construction, rough ends and edges, and leather straps for hinges and latches. The primitive worker used what he had at hand.

PLATE 6–20

EARLY SIX-MAN PUMPER

Although this item is not a piece of furniture, it has been included in the book to illustrate that the same techniques used in restoring furniture may also be applied to other types of restoration. The early firefighting equipment shown here was found in an old cheese factory in Brownstown, Illinois. Except for the wheels, which had rotted away because the pumper had been stored on a dirt floor, all parts to the wagon are original. The pumps were completely reworked and made operable. The large brass bell on the side of the tank clangs with each rotation of the wheels. The body of the wagon is actually a water tank to be filled by a bucket brigade. A valve inside the tank allows water to be pumped either from the onboard tank, or from some outside source such as a well.

PLATE 6–21

Manufacturer's tag for an early piece of firefighting equipment.

Index